CW01669883

CULT OF THE SACRED SPEAR

Cult of the Sacred Spear

The story of the Nuer Tribe in Ethiopia

BRIAN HUGH MACDERMOT

ROBERT HALE · LONDON

© Brian Hugh MacDermot 1972
First published in Great Britain 1972

ISBN 0 7091 3291 3

Robert Hale & Company
63 Old Brompton Road
London S.W.7

Printed in Great Britain by
Willmer Brothers Limited, Birkenhead

Contents

Appendices

Illustrations

Acknowledgements

I would like to thank the Nuer without whom this book would not have been written; also my various and long suffering secretaries who have, on occasions, all helped: Miss Margaret Tweedie, Miss Jennifer Clark and Miss Lindsay Parsons. In Ethiopia H.I.H. The Crown Prince, the British Ambassador at the time, John Russell, Ato Hapte Selassie and John Blower. I shall always be grateful to Thomas Mattanovitch for his kindness and assistance.

In London Dr Richard Gray, Aubrey Buxton, John Hillaby and Wilfred Thesiger. In Oxford, Professor Sir Edward Evans-Pritchard, Dr Godfrey Lienhardt, and the late Dr Jean Buxton—all of whom offered me encouragement.

TO THE NUER

Nuer Dramatis Personnae

DOEREDING	Nuer interpreter who accompanied the author throughout his trip
GAR QUOT	Appointed chief of Gwal Diok and head of the local judiciary
THIWAT	Adopted son of Gar Quot, actually a nephew. He assisted the author
KIIR	Another assistant who did the cooking and proved a devoted disciple
NYATHIANG	Owner of the hut occupied by the author whilst in Gwal Diok
KOR JUM WIU	Prophet of Wiu, God of the Sacred Spear
MUONY	The 'gaar' or man who carried out 'garring' (the cutting of heads)
KOR JUM DENG	Prophet of Deng, God of Fertility
RIAL NYANG	The author

Brief Nuer Vocabulary

(Terms used in this book)

Anya-Nya	Freedom fighters in the South Sudan
Biel	Nuer spirit
Buk	Nuer spirit of the river (fishing)
Chot	Boys during the period of isolation following 'garring'
Coat	The period of isolation after 'garring'
Deng	God of Fertility
Gaar	The man who performs 'garring'
Gar	Tribal mark on forehead
Garring	The act of cutting the foreheads, maturity ceremony
Jang	Slave, foreigner (such as Dinka)
Kuoth Nhial	The spirits above
Kiir	God of Origin, the Nile
Male	Greeting (or *Male MiGwa, Male MiDit* etc.)
Maluth	Nuer spirit
Muot	Final marriage ceremony and collection of the bride by the groom
Ngut	Main marriage ceremony
Nyang	Crocodile, also refers to a mixed colour brown and white
Rial	Multicoloured
Wiu	God of the Sacred Spear
Wutni	The status of manhood
Yoat	Period of engagement before marriage

Preface

What I have done is to try to tell a true story relating to myself and a tribe—or, at least, a small part of a tribe. This visit may not be everyone's idea of a perfect holiday, but at least, like a cold shower on a wintry morning, it proved all the more pleasant once it was over. Pleasure in reminiscence is not only the privilege of age. In writing, I have fallen between two stools—this is neither a serious anthropological survey, nor an exciting personal drama embellished, as so many writers have often done, by exaggeration, if not by down-right lies. Instead, this story incorporates what I believe to be some valid facts about the Nuer. Not being a qualified anthropologist, I could hardly hope to do more.

On the travel story side, I have tried to write with complete candour and truth. If some of the events have lost their original chronological sequence it is mainly due to the fact that I kept no notes at the time and had to rely on memory. Remember too I was a single white man with a native interpreter, struggling to survive in a totally strange environment. Nor was I often idle, for besides administering medical aid, I was frequently tape recording, shooting film for television or taking still photographs. Add to all this the fact that my time was limited and perhaps the critics may find a kindly work for what was achieved. At any rate, I had proved to myself that a 40-year-old bachelor can tear himsef away from the City for a brief period to live quite happily without the comforts of modern civilization. Moreover, I had also proved that it was possible to become almost totally accepted by a primitive people. The measure of such acceptance may never be known, but I hope that, at least, a few of the Nuer will, when we next meet, remember me as I remember them—as good friends.

Some background notes on the war in South Sudan have been provided in the form of Appendices. Appendix 1 gives a political resumé covering the last few years, whilst Appendix 2 shows how the situation arose in the view of a retired British governor of one of the provinces. Appendices 3 and 4 deal with events under the Nimeiri government. Appendix 5 mentions negotiations going on at present between North and South Sudan. Since the political history of the Sudan would otherwise have interrupted the narrative, it has been isolated in this way.

The Garden of Eden

CHAPTER I

"Thirteen months of sunshine" read the posters as I settled aboard a Boeing 707 bound for Addis Ababa and the kingdom of His Imperial Majesty Haile Selassie, Lion of Judah, King of Kings.

This was to be my second trip to Ethiopia. My previous visit had been to the heart of the Danakil Country. The Danakil are a ferocious tribe who frequently castrate their enemies and sometimes wear the trophies obtained in this manner around their necks as a decoration. These Muslims are much feared by the rest of Ethiopia. Exactly one year ago, in the company of John Blower, the Chief Game Warden of the area, I had explored from Awash to Tendaho and eastwards across the desert, counting game and getting to know the tribes.

We had followed in the footsteps of many explorers, yet this did not lessen the excitement of entering forbidden territory where sultans rule with medieval ferocity, chopping off hands of thieves and hanging other offenders. Nesbitt, covering the same ground half a century ago, encountered incredible dangers, losing most of his men, and was lucky to emerge alive.

This time I hoped to go the furthest I could on untrodden paths, entering the territory of the Nuer, a pagan tribe often studied by anthropologists but seldom visited. I had read references to their religious customs, which intrigued me and I decided to try to examine their culture. On such a trip a white hunter is nearly always necessary. He provides the tents, vehicles, guns and other equipment—as well as protecting the life of his client in the wilds.

John Blower was on the tarmac to meet me, and take me to the Ghion Hotel, where I was to meet the white hunter he had engaged on my behalf. Thomas Mattanovitch was a thin young man of about 28, with wild eyes and a smile which appeared in fits and starts. Originally he had come from Yugoslavia with his family, but he had been brought up mainly in Ethiopia. I had never encountered a white hunter quite like Thomas. At this, our first meeting in the Ghion Hotel bar, I thought that the last thing in the world I would do would be to entrust my life to him by going on a joint safari. At one moment he was so vague that any form of organization would obviously be quite beyond his powers. At the next he would tell such boastful stories about killing three-legged men living in trees that it was equally obvious one could not believe a word he said. Nevertheless John had assured me that this man was a first-class hunter—but more important still he was the beloved son of many of the Anuak peoples who inhabit the Province of Illubador, part of Western Ethiopia.

After a rather sticky dinner at the Ghion Hotel we left to do a tour of the night spots of Addis. It has been estimated that there are more prostitutes in Addis Ababa than in any other city in the world, though it would surprise me if Tokyo did not run a close second. These girls of leisure forgather in the evenings in the 'tedj halls' and there the happy tourist, for the modest price of a few Ethiopian dollars, can savour both the *tedj* (a form of mead more alcoholic than is at first supposed) and the company and companionship of large Ethiopian women dressed in the national costume of white robes with green borders. We decided to visit a well-known night club called the 'Queen of Sheba'. Inside the drums beat rhythmically, there was a smell of sweat as Africans gyrated to the latest music and a few attractive girls lounged listlessly at the bar. Dim lighting came from lamps sunk into the floor or hidden behind the bar, but not so dim that one could not see the skins of illegally killed monkeys covering the walls of the club. There must have been hundreds of them and they gave the place a sinister appearance. We were soon surrounded by a crowd of Ethiopians in smart suits with elegantly dressed female consorts. As we drank brandy at the bar, keeping an eye on the girls on the dance floor, Thomas and I established a 'rapport' which was to last throughout our forthcoming venture. He loved life, liked people, adored animals but loathed planning. It was with such an unexpected companion and with an awful hangover that I set out the next morning in the small plane heading from Addis to Gambela in the Western province of Illubador.

After frequent stops during which both live and dead cargo were shuttled on and off the aeroplane—(a goat with its feet tied together spending most of its time under my seat)—we arrived at Gambela, in the westernmost part of Ethiopia and situated on the Baro River. To me it was to represent the Garden of Eden—a natural oasis in an often unhospitable land. I suppose the Garden of Eden should be a place where everything works out perfectly, but in our case we arrived with a considerable amount of baggage at the airport to find that the only way of reaching the town, some 2 or 3 miles away, would be to walk there carrying our possessions. After enlisting the services of a number of the Anuak to help us with our baggage we covered the distance, arriving at a miserable looking tin shack announced as Thomas's house. As the door was opened a couple of chickens fled the interior whilst startled screams came from an Anuak girl previously lying naked on the one and only bed in the room. "My cook", said Thomas, with the air of a lord and master effecting a necessary introduction.

On seeing a stranger she had flung a sheet around herself and stood there looking like a princess. She was a beautiful girl with ivory rings on her arms, a flat nose and an aristocratic bearing. She was devoted to Thomas, although lacking a few European refinements such as using a handkerchief or bothering with plates and cutlery when she served us food. Nevertheless she turned out to be willing and helpful as well as full of good humour, except when attacked by Thomas's pet baboon. This crude animal made a habit of diving under womens' skirts—to the great amusement of male onlookers.

It is hard to describe Gambela as a town. It could perhaps more correctly be called a collection of mud and tin huts spread over a limited area. A few generators supply electricity to one or two buildings such as the government offices and the Sudanese Consulate. But elsewhere there is no electricity, no plumbing and very little attempt to dispose of refuse. Owing to the number of refugees from the Sudan, who had fled to Ethiopia (see Appendices 1–4 for an explanation of the war in the Sudan) this village was vastly overcrowded, with men, women and children sleeping on the ground everywhere or just sitting in the streets. The roads had long since fallen into ill repair but one could see that they were once the pride of an outpost of the British Empire, for strangely enough Gambela was formerly a British free port—i.e. a trading post situated on the borders of the Sudan and Ethiopia. The streets had once been laid out in perfect squares with whitewashed stones. Some of these stones could still be seen lying in heaps, a memorial to the past.

As we were wandering through the town two Ethiopian policemen came up behind us, and Thomas and I were hustled away without ceremony or explanation towards a barbed wire compound in the centre of the town. Some of the local inhabitants looked on with apprehension for they had all learned to fear the police, not always known for their gentle behaviour in outlying posts. At the station, I was cross-questioned by an obviously panic-stricken officer. He had me searched by his men and then, much to Thomas's fury, we were both thrown into a small airless room, the door being bolted from outside.

Now I am not very keen on prisons, particularly African ones, which normally provide no food, it being the custom for a wife or relations to cook for you whilst 'inside'. Twice before I had been locked up—once in the Congo on the Northern Rhodesian border, and once on a previous visit to Ethiopia while on the way back from Awash. On the first occasion, I had been able to argue my way out by convincing the border guards that I was not a spy; and on the second I was in the good company of John Blower when we were accused of shooting oryx—an animal protected in the game reserves by order of the Emperor. Of course, we had done no such thing, but, owing to our refusal to pay the normal bribe of 10 Ethiopian dollars to the game guard stationed at a road barrier, he had in pique reported us, little realizing that he was locking up his own boss! All could then have been settled had the game guard restricted himself to calling in one district governor. In fact, to gain additional kudos, he had called up two, which resulted in nothing less than a battle to gain possession of the prisoners. The Governor of Nazareth eventually won over the Governor of Dire Dawa and we were shipped off to prison there. On arrival we were treated as important guests and after several hours of discussion we were freed—after all, the police only needed to examine the skull and skin of our Summering gazelle to see it was not an oryx or anything like it—the horns for one thing being of a totally different shape, curved instead of straight.

To return to the arrest in Gambela. Neither Thomas nor I knew what the charges against us were—nor, it appeared, did the police. They had received a wireless message to say that I—yes, it was the same name or something like it, 'Macdiamud'—was to be locked up. Thomas seemed to have been taken in for good measure. Once we were safely locked up, the chief of police was able to call Addis at his leisure and ask for further instructions.

After what seemed like hours, we were released and I was told that I was to fetch my machine gun! What had happened was that, whilst 'en route' for Gambela, I had been using my bolex cine camera with a zoom lens. At one of the plane's frequent stops for refuelling someone must have mistaken the camera for a machine gun and reported the incident to the police. It was not until the camera had been produced, its contents thoroughly examined, the film being exposed in the process, that the mistake was discovered amidst guffaws of laughter. All very well for the police to think it was a good joke—but we had been roughed up, pushed into an

0 Miles 50
R. Sobat
Nasir
NUER
Jakaw
Dembidola
Lare
Gwal Diok
Gambela
Teleuth
Wiu
R. Baro
Itang
SUDAN
ANUAK
ETHIOPIA
R. Pibor
R. Gilo
Inset of shaded area below
Nile
NORTHER
KORDOFAN
DARFUR
SUDA
White Nile
Mala
SHILLUK
UPPER NILE
BAHR EL GHAZAL
DINKA
Wau
DINKA BOR
CENTRAL AFRICAN REPUBLIC
EQUATO
CONGO
UG
Capital
Town
Village
International bdy.
Provincial bdy.
Tribal names NUER
0 Miles 200

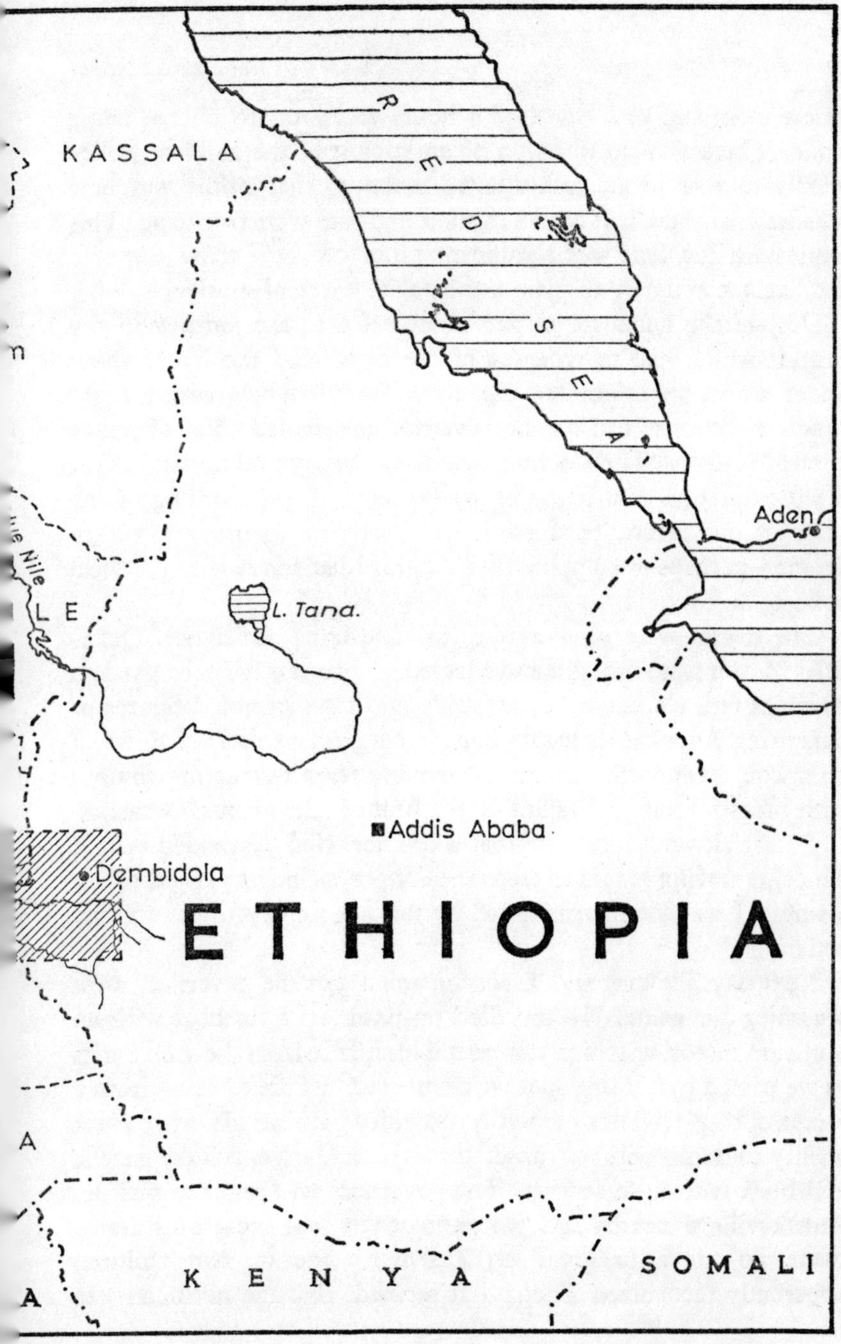

KASSALA
RED SEA
Aden
L. Tana.
Addis Ababa
Dembidola
ETHIOPIA
KENYA
SOMALI

airless room and kept waiting for hours without any charge being made. There was no question of an apology, the chief of police merely told us in an authoritative manner that Addis was now satisfied that there had been a mistake and we were free to go. This unpleasant incident was significant proof of how tense the area had become and how suspicious the police were of strangers.

Despite the hangover of the night before, the journey in the aircraft which had taken most of the day, and the hours spent under arrest, we celebrated our arrival in Gambela with a night dance. A courtesy call on the governor, an exiled chief of police known locally as 'The Colonel', was a necessary preliminary. After the presentation of a bottle of whisky and the recounting of the story of our arrest, permission was granted to use the village drums—perhaps in compensation for our lost hours with the local police.

The drums were soon beating to announce our dance. Quantities of beer were brought and a large bonfire was lit in the garden. As night fell, clothes were cast aside and the splended figures of perspiring Anuak girls leapt about in suggestive dances. Rows of girls would approach and retreat moving to a fascinating rhythm with breasts rising and falling to the beat of the drums. Occasionally a shriek would indicate that a brother had descended on the dance, removing his sister from the danger of being carried off by a suitor. I was soon mesmerized by this scene of almost orgiastic activity.

Next day Thomas and I, accompanied by the governor, went searching for game. We travelled up-river in a tin boat with an outboard motor, watching the crocodile slither from the sand banks as we passed by. At one spot we clambered ashore to drink from a secret spring which supposedly provided the locals with great virility and me with an upset tummy. We also chased gazelle and buck with little success. The governor was eager to visit an Anuak village nearby. As we approached the local inhabitants made no move to greet us, although one or two children apparently recognized Thomas. It seemed that the headman was away, so one of his brothers came to question us. Somewhat put out by his inability to exercise his authority, the governor demanded an account of the arms retained and the taxes paid by the villagers. Since nobody appeared to know what on earth he was talking about, the meeting became decidedly unpleasant. It was only after Thomas managed to talk to the people in local dialect that we were able to leave peaceably.

If I had had any doubts before about the reception of Amhara from Addis Ababa (even powerful ones) by the local inhabitants of the area, these were now resolved. The Amhara have for centuries been the rulers of Ethiopia. The government and police (nearly all Amhara) are merely tolerated as long as they remain remote. Throughout Ethiopia it has always been apparent that obedience to the Emperor and his representatives is voluntary. It is the magic of the name Haile Selassie which holds the Ethiopian nations together. Arabs and Bantu, Nilots and Coptic Christians, and above all the Amharic peoples, all owe some form of allegiance to His Imperial Majesty.

On the return journey Thomas played a tom, an Anuak musical instrument. His thumbs moved across small pieces of metal attached to a hollowed wooden base. A twanging sound of great charm emerged, as we drifted downstream. Occasionally native Anuak would rush to the bank of the river displaying small children as we passed by shouting, "Thomas, this is one of yours." This happened so many times that I began to wonder if they were really his offspring or whether perhaps his reputation for conquest of Anuak maidens had outstripped actual performance. Thomas swore it was all lies and the girls were just trying to get money out of him.

For days we lounged around Gambela attempting to buy supplies, with my white hunter generally forgetting either the money or to collect the goods after purchase. The whole operation was so incredibly vague and disorganized that I became irritated and accused Thomas of wasting time on purpose. He was deeply offended and suggested that we should call off the expedition unless I could be brought to realize that in Africa there was no such thing as time. No one must be hurried! Moreover, Thomas appeared to be involved in so many local disputes with the governor and the police, that I was constantly afraid lest he should be arrested again before we could even start our trip. I never could get to the bottom of his disputes, which nearly all involved such mundane subjects as paying rent (or not paying it). There was also the question of buying petrol from the government stores. This would certainly have been impossible but for the kindness of the governor, who had decided that he was going to do everything he could to help us.

Contact with the Nuer

CHAPTER 2

"We know not what to do; we are at a loss. Deng, spirits of the above, save this child. We have no eyes, the family of Nijapuka obeys blindly. Forgive the family and the child—save the child from death."

(Nuer spirits speaking through a possessed woman.)

When the tin boat, piled with tents and stores, together with four Anuak, Thomas and myself, finally headed down river I could hardly believe that at last we were on our way. Thomas sang some Yugoslav song to the crocodiles; the outboard motor purred away. I sat feeling as if I were the commander of the *African Queen* with a black sombrero on my head, feet dangling in the water as crocodile bait. Our Anuak companions were two elderly camp 'boys' and two young learners who were being trained for safari work. At our first stop, an Anuak village some 10 miles distant, the two learners changed their minds about coming any further and remained in the village. One of the elderly Anuak also suddenly developed stomach pains which made it impossible for him to continue. Thus, within two hours of starting we lost 75 per cent of our crew. Doubtless this was all my fault for I had foolishly told our team that I wanted to visit the Nuer. This tribe was well known for its ferocity and feared by the Anuak who had fought them for centuries. Presumably, therefore, it was the mention of the Nuer that had caused these desertions. There remained with us one rather sour-looking elderly Anuak.

As we progressed down river frequent stops were made for Thomas to visit the villages we passed. There was inevitably an urgent reason to stop. There was always an equally good reason to spend as long as possible drinking and talking with the local inhabitants. The story was often the same—the troops, both Ethiopian and Sudanese, had been there (see Appendices 1–5 for explanation of the Sudanese war), the crops had been burnt, they had no weapons to protect themselves, and a number of sick needed treatment. For two days we travelled down river at this unvaryingly slow pace whilst I became excessively impatient with the prolonged conferences. Occasionally we called at Ethiopian police posts and I would present my credentials registering my name, although I was quite certain that nobody would ever know or care what on earth I was doing in this remote part of the world.

There was one village which stands out in my memory. It was governed by an excessively handsome young Anuak chieftain with long finger nails and an almost feminine manner. He was beautifully dressed and groomed as he walked with great dignity to the shore to greet us. Then to my amazement in front of all his followers he prostrated himself on the ground kissing Thomas's feet. Evidently his father had been a particular friend of Thomas's and when the old man died he had nominated Thomas as the spiritual leader of his people.

Although we were given a splendid reception, all was not well with the village; the natives seemed to be forcing smiles on their faces. There then took place a conference to end all conferences, lasting the best part of five hours.

A band of the southern Sudanese rebels known as 'Anya-Nya' had moved into the village requesting food and shelter from the inhabitants. After they had left, only two days before our arrival, a punitive police raid had taken place: the crops were burned; then the chieftain and elders were tied to trees and beaten with rhino whips; all the food in the village was confiscated and it was demanded that all weapons should be handed in immediately.

The proof of the harsh treatment handed out, remained not only on the back of the chieftain (who showed us the horrible wounds he had suffered) but also on the stomachs of the villagers. The village had now used up even the small quantities of food the women had been able to hide away. With no crops they would certainly starve within a month.

Thomas questioned the elders and discovered that the village was hiding an arsenal of weapons which they supplied to the rebels. These weapons were hidden in an underground pit which we were eventually taken to see. The Ethiopian police must have had some knowledge of these bren guns, mortars, rifles and ammunition—wanting them for themselves. Thomas, with the wisdom of Solomon, decided that there was only one solution. We loaded their canoes with some of the arms and ammunition and told the elders to go up river to Itang to hand over the consignment to the police in exchange for the food and grain (or what was left of it) which had been confiscated. The rest of the weapons were again buried outside the village. Later we heard that the police were delighted at acquiring new and valuable weapons, and the villagers for their part were equally pleased to be able to remain in their village growing their crops certain of survival for another season. The fact that they had retained the majority of their weapons would mean that they could still assist the cause which was obviously so close to their hearts, that of supporting the rebel army which was fighting in South Sudan.

Late that evening as we drifted on downstream the crocodiles yawned baring their teeth and birds of many colours skimmed past us on the surface of the water.

The sun had almost set when we decided to seek hospitality in a small Anuak Village before continuing towards the homelands of the Nuer, which we were now approaching. As always Anuak came rushing to greet us; drums were soon beating to announce a dance. It was in this village I first saw some members of the Nuer tribe, easily distinguished by the marks on their foreheads cut during a special maturity ceremony called garring (See Chapter 10). They wore no clothes but looked much like the Anuak except for their tribal marks. The Anuak asked two of these visiting Nuer, whom they trusted, if they would be willing to take us to their village the next day and they agreed.

The Anuak continued with their dancing, singing songs about the glory of their royal house and relating the saga of the sacred beads. The Anuak love bright colours, prizing above all else blue beads which are supposed to have come from some sacred source. Indeed it is impossible to marry without these beads and they tend to be regarded as family heirlooms. Once again we watched the Anuak girls dancing rhythmically with the moonlight shining on their perspiring bodies and reflecting off the ivory bands on their wrists and arms. Their dark skin mingled with the blackness of the night whilst the two-toned drums continued to beat out their messages of love and war. Long after we had retired for the night the drums continued to beat. Occasionally a weird wail or screech would be heard—we were told this represented Nuer singing. Tomorrow, with luck, we would reach the Nuer tribe, the object of my trip.

Long before the sun rose a young Nuer boy aged about 6 or 7 woke us, announcing that he was ready to go to his village. He had been sent by the two Nuer we had met the previous night. As we had brought a considerable amount of camping equipment it was necessary to pay some Anuak to help us carry the loads. Eventually the services of about a dozen Anuak men and women were enlisted. They would walk with us most of the day into the swamps carrying tents and supplies on their heads; the fee being settled at approximately 25p per head.

It was several hours before we were under way, mainly because the men argued endlessly with their companions as to who was to carry what. It ended up that anything heavy had to be carried by one of the women—the men selecting for themselves something nice and easy such as my Leica camera. A young Anuak boy aged about 12, who was covered with beads and wore a number of feathers in his hair, had attached himself to me and insisted on coming on the trip, although I explained that he would not be paid.

He was a sort of a 'Beau Brummel' of the village, endlessly flirting with all the girls. The object of attaching himself to me soon became apparent when he frequently invited me to part with my watch or other items of clothing or adornment.

Most of the day was spent wading through the swamps with leeches clinging to our legs, in the most appalling heat. As the swamp got deeper those Anuak who had any clothes on took them off, carrying the bundles on their heads together with our burdens. As we frequently sank up to our arms in mud and water, I followed their example, thus providing Thomas with a chance to photograph a naked stockbroker slithering through the mud and water attempting to maintain both balance and dignity much to the amusement of the local porters. (I believe this photograph is still shown in Addis as proof of the craziness of Englishmen visiting foreign countries.)

As we trudged through this impossible countryside, I became more and more horrified by the number of leeches I was collecting. I could not help imagining that they must be removing my blood in such quantities that it would run out. As soon as I lit a cigarette and burnt them off, the next swamp would appear and the whole process would begin all over again. These little animals arrive so quietly that you never feel them there in the first place. It is only when you emerge from the water that you find them sticking to you in unexpected places.

We were utterly exhausted when we finally approached the Nuer village, having crossed what seemed like miles of endless swamp land. Leeches had sucked my blood, mosquitoes had bitten me all over and the strong rays of the sun left me with a beetroot-like complexion. A cluster of huts could now be seen rising out of the swamps. Cattle browsed amongst the reeds, as Nuer warriors came out of their homes and gathered around these strange visitors, while the women and children at first hid inside their huts. The Nuer men all had cuts on their foreheads, some more marked than others. They were tall—many well over 6 foot—and nearly all were completely naked. Spears were held in their right hands whilst one or two carried leather shields. As they ran towards us the welcome appeared anything but friendly, some jostled us, others shouted, both at us and our guides. Our Anuak porters decided they had had enough and demanding their money took off at a trot across the swamp to head back to their own territory. Our baggage was thus left in disorderly piles under a large tree on the outskirts of the village. It remained to be seen if these Nuer would let us stay.

By now the entire village had turned up. Thomas asked for the local headman who came slowly forward scowling and grunting; obviously he disapproved of our visit, which could only cause him trouble in that he might be held responsible for stolen goods or if any harm came to us. However, he decided to make the best of an awkward situation and allowed us to stay, provided we camped outside the village itself and kept a constant guard on our possessions. Most of this discussion was carried out by hand signs, much to the amusement of onlookers. As the sun was now setting and it would soon be dark, I started organizing our camp under the large tree where our equipment had been left by the Anuak. With a burst of energy I attempted to chop down some of the overhanging branches of this tree with my 'Wilkinson Sword' jungle knife, in order to clear an area for our tent. This proved to be doubly unfortunate, firstly because the tree happened to be sacred and was worshipped by this particular band of Nuer as we found out later, and secondly, because the blade of my knife flew off its handle, whistled across the arena and narrowly missed the son of the chief. There was a moment of silence before I fully realized what had happened. Luckily the Nuer considered the breaking of the knife evidence of the power of their sacred tree, and since the chief's son was unharmed everyone agreed to forget the incident. But it was hardly an auspicious introduction.

What first struck me about the Nuer as they gathered around to watch Thomas and myself pitching our tents was the gaping sores on their arms and legs. These were raw open wounds, sometimes several inches in diameter; the entire village was suffering from yaws! The disease is somewhat similar to syphilis although it can be transmitted by touch or water. To Africans it is highly infectious, although Europeans are believed to be immune. As the wounds grow larger so they tend to cripple, the virus eating into the bone and causing intense pain. Once a village becomes badly infected, as this one was, it is almost impossible to cure the population without a large supply of medicine. Penicillin is certainly the answer, but when this is lacking, as it was in our case, we employed and old missionary technique of boiling butter and applying it with leaves in a form of hot compress bandaged on to the wound. Strangely enough after a few days the wounds began to heal partially and this success brought an endless procession of the sick from miles around to our tent.

Since neither Thomas nor I spoke Nuer and there was no one to interpret for us, it was difficult to understand what was happening or to make any real contact with the people. I felt constantly frustrated by being separated from them, living outside their village and unable to communicate. Moreover, being in a tent made us somehow different. Europeans on safari are often isolated from the native peoples with whom they come into contact. I realized if I were ever to get to know the Nuer properly I should have to come again on another visit.

Thomas and I tended the sick, watched the Nuer dancing and occasionally tried to quiz them by signs and signals about their customs and religion. One evening a Nuer, called Benjamin, who spoke a few words of English arrived at our camp bringing a chicken. After we had feasted, he invited us to come up to the village where he said "God has arrived". It was late; dogs barked as we approached and Benjamin led the way to a hut in the centre where a number of Nuer were praying to their gods. An old man was standing in the middle of a circle of worshippers, letting forth an occasional high-pitched scream which was answered by those surrounding him singing in unison. After about an hour and just as I was begining to get bored, there was a sudden change in tempo, the prayers being repeated with greater rapidity. A new voice was heard taking the lead and I thought that someone was calling to a spirit called 'Gwot'. It was only afterwards that Benjamin explained what had happened. Beneath a cloth cover a woman was rolling on the ground possessed by the spirits, and shouting to the gods. She had, according to Benjamin, uttered the words of god telling the people what they should do to avoid the sickness which had hit the village. The most extraordinary aspect of this strange ceremony was that while the woman was possessed, she started to speak in a husky male voice bearing no resemblance to her own. Since I had my tape-recorder with me I recorded the words she shouted and had them translated a year later by a Nuer friend in London. She was a woman in her late 50s a wizened little creature who normally spoke in a high-pitched wail. Later when she visited our camp I played back her words on the tape-recorder and she was truly amazed to hear herself speaking while possessed. "Deng God of Earth—forgive the child—though the family must sacrifice—Each spirit of the above be with us, with the might and power of Wiu—for we all lack eyes and owe obedience etc. . . ."

At the time the words meant nothing to me, I was still completely ignorant about the religion and customs of the Nuer, but my curiosity had been sufficiently roused by this first brief and rather unsatisfactory visit to ensure my return. In the meantime I would do as much research on the tribe as was possible in London so that when I returned I would be in a better position to get to know them, in spite of not speaking their language.

Time was now running out. We had been with the Nuer for ten days, and I would soon be due back at work in England, whilst Thomas had other clients coming. The return journey across the swamps, up river to Gambela and thence by plane to Addis was uneventful. Back in Addis Ababa itself I made enquiries about the political situation of the Sudanese tribes in an attempt to understand why the Khartoum government was driving them out of their homelands. The Ethiopian authorities were certainly worried about the increasing number of Sudanese refugees crossing their borders. But at that time (namely 1967) the refugees were not

Setting out to find the Nuer

(*above*) Thomas Mattanc vitch. (*left*) Thomas's Anua cook during the author' first visit.

officially recognized by the government, so no protests had been made. Moreover the Nuer were well-known as a migratory tribe of pastoralists so that it would be difficult to prove that their arrival in large numbers in Ethiopia was anything other than a temporary embarrassment. In this situation I found Ethiopian government officials reluctant to talk about the Sudan, fearing perhaps to increase the breach with their neighbouring state. It was remarkable how this war in the Sudan had failed to hit the headlines then.

As regards the Nuer I had met, they were certainly refugees in the sense that they had crossed the borders out of the Sudan into Ethiopia—but so far their life had not changed much, apart from the lack of medicine and education which some time before had been provided by a British administration. Soon the Nuer would be fighting to survive not only against an often hostile environment but also against the modern weapons of a foreign-equipped army from Khartoum. My next visit was to show how swiftly the situation deteriorated. (See also Appendices 1–5).

No White Hunter

CHAPTER 3

You, the sons of foreigners, you will be surrounded by us
Should you come to meet us, it will be death.
If you wait and hide away, it will be death.
So make your choice which way you die!
Your cattle belong to us and your children will not drink the milk
For the milk will be drunk by warriors, ourselves.

(Nuer War Song.)

It was almost a year and a half later before I was able to return to the Nuer. During the intervening period I had done some work of a semi anthropological nature. In England there was one outstanding expert on the customs of the Nuer, Sir Edward Evans-Pritchard, Professor of Social Anthropology at Oxford University. Evans-Pritchard had written three excellent works as well as numerous articles on the Nuer based on his experiences during the early 1930s. As one of the founders of modern social anthropology, he had collected a vast amount of information about the tribe which amounted to a complete account of their life in all its aspects*. What was hard to estimate was the accuracy of some of his findings. One could not help being left with the impression that he had carried out much of his research by means of a series of interviews conducted in his tent. This impression was confirmed when during a brief interview I met the professor at Oxford. He was decidedly startled by my suggestion that he might have enjoyed dancing with

* See *The Nuer*, 1940, *Kinship and Marriage amongst the Nuer*, 1951, and *Nuer Religion*, 1956, by E. E. Evans-Pritchard (Clarendon Press, Oxford).

the tribe or eating their food. He did not indicate to me then that this had been the method of his more serious research.

It remains true that without the advantages of Evans-Pritchard's research, there would have been no basis for anyone else to carry out further investigation. Reading his books enabled me, for instance, to understand some of the customs of the tribe and awakened my power of observation so that seemingly unimportant incidents all fell into a pattern. Unfortunately no really modern comprehensive work has been done on the Nuer, although studies have been made on certain aspects of their life such as Nuer law.

Anthropological study was therefore to be the prime motive of my next visit. Secondly I wanted to find out what effect the war in the Sudan was having on the tribes and what could be done about it, at least in so far as aid to refugees was concerned. In England little interest was exhibited, and indeed little was generally known about the political situation in South Sudan. Television companies which I approached indicated that they would be interested in any film material on the war, but were not prepared to finance an expedition. Finally a young doctor who was a close friend of mine said she would come with me on the next trip to help the sick. A three-fold objective was established (always fatal)—namely anthropology, filming and medical aid.

The second visit was to be perfectly organized! As time was of the greatest importance, not a moment was to be wasted. The importance of time was stressed in telegrams to Thomas, and he was urged to reserve the month of May 1968 to lead the expedition. Even before setting off things began to go wrong. The doctor failed the final part of her Membership of the Royal College of Physicians and was unable to come; the television companies decided in the end not to send a photographer as I had hoped, but to leave the whole of the filming and cost to me; and Thomas did not reply to any of my telegrams.

No sooner had my aeroplane landed at Addis Ababa than I discovered that my white hunter had disappeared into the bush some months before and no one had any news of him. My safari which had been ordered a year ahead and so carefully planned with trucks and tents and equipment, all to be ready in the area required, appeared to have got inexorably tied up in the normal chaos of Ethiopian red tape. After waiting a few days in Addis I decided to head for Gambela in the hope of finding Thomas.

After three days in Gambela I only managed to discover that the adventurous Thomas had last been seen shooting crocodile in the Ghilo river together with some Germans. I learnt later that he had left the crossing of the river too late in the year, when due to the early rains the water was in full flood, and he had attempted to float his trucks across. The result was not only the temporary loss of a truck but also the complete loss of his supplies of food and the eventual breakdown of his vehicle convoy. Berthe, Thomas's Amharic female cook had tried to save the situation by driving the one remaining working vehicle at full speed towards Gambela in an attempt to reach the client—namely myself. Not being a skilled driver, she had, alas, only succeeded in progressing a mile or two before crashing the Land-Rover into a tree and breaking the steering.

So while I waited for news in Gambela with growing impatience, Thomas was somewhere the far side of the Ghilo river attempting to mend his vehicles and maintain the broken morale of his camp and cook! I had despatched at least half a dozen runners in all directions to search for him—each carrying a letter which they were instructed to give the white hunter. I was to learn later that after running for four days one of these messengers did in fact reach Thomas who had opened and read the following communication from myself "Am awaiting safari in Gambela. Come as quickly as possible. If you fail to reach Gambela during the first week in May, head for Teleuth". Thomas is said to have torn up the message, roaring with laughter at the thought of being able, at that moment to move in any direction. His main concern then was the rescue and repair of his vehicles combined with the desire to get himself and his party to safety as soon as possible.

Meanwhile in Gambela I discovered that there was nowhere to

stay except the local brothel. Being somewhat loath to spend much time in this noisy and unpleasant place, it was with relief that I met and was invited to stay with Dr McConnell of the American Naval mission. This kindly, quiet doctor, a parasitologist or expert on mosquitoes and other parasites, was highly amused by my plans and eager to help me re-organize my safari. Various Nuer in Gambela were contacted to find an interpreter. (There were now several hundred Nuer refugees who had come as far as the town.) Finally the most unlikely character arrived. His name was Doereding and to this day I have not forgotten his strange appearance at Dr McConnell's house.

We were contentedly eating mangoes on the porch of this one European-type dwelling, when Doereding came up to us carrying a battered umbrella. He had a round face, permanently blood-shot eyes (I suspected from drink) and an often truculent expression. From time to time this disappeared as he chuckled with delight. In perfect English he introduced himself and said he understood that there was someone who wished to visit his people; that he, Doereding, might be willing to escort him. Doereding wanted to go to the Teleuth area for two or three days to visit relatives and then hurry back to town where his wife had just produced a child. He was, he explained, an old man (he was 42) and did not want to spend much time in the discomfort of the bush. He also told us he had a very beautiful cook in Gambela whom he did not wish to leave for long. He explained that he had a "fascination with politics" and had originally been elected to parliament in Khartoum, only to be arrested by the police in South Sudan before he had been able to take his seat. Doereding was also in trouble with the Ethiopian police and this was an additional reason why he would be glad to get out of Gambela for a while. He claimed the Sudanese Consul there was attempting to get him arrested, extradited as a political prisoner and returned to Khartoum for trial.

When Doereding left Dr McConnell's house he had agreed to join me the next day, although my plan of remaining a month with the Nuer at Teleuth was longer than he originally wanted.

I was somewhat startled by several Nuer boys, including Dr McConnell's right-hand mosquito man, David (the boy entrusted to catch and bottle mosquitoes for future laboratory tests), saying that Doereding was evil and not to be trusted. However, having read how each clan of Nuer tends to mistrust its neighbour, it seemed to me possible that David and his friends had some tribal reason for disliking Doereding. I thought it better to trust my own judgement.

It was with some trepidation that I set out from Gambela with, as my only guide a Nuer rebel gaol bird who was clearly 'wanted' in a number of places. Nor did Doereding's capacity for organizing reassure me. He appeared for the start of our journey one hour late and with no other equipment or food beyond his one umbrella with its broken spokes and a couple of mangoes for his lunch. He explained he had no money and indeed no clothes or goods since he was sure I would look after him. For my part I had discovered that Gambela was pretty well out of food, and beyond buying a couple of bottles of whisky and a few tins of fruit, I thought that any attempt to provision myself properly would be a waste of time. If I were going to visit the Nuer, I would have to rely on being accepted by them and either purchasing, or in some other way obtaining, food and drink. Doereding did not seem over-worried and assured me that he had many friends in the Teleuth area.

As we set off on the first lap of the journey, both of us sitting in the back of an old truck heading for the police post at Itang, there was a cheerful atmosphere of adventure. The most intrepid explorer tends to disintegrate after a couple of hours of being bumped around in the back of a vegetable truck with nothing to protect him from the rays of the scorching sun. An Indian driver had taken us aboard as fare-paying passengers (£1 each for a 50-mile journey). As the dust filled our lungs, we were jolted against the hard metallic sides of the vehicle.

At Itang the last police formalities were undertaken. Religiously an illiterate captain of police recorded the details of my 'passport'. In fact, I had left my passport behind and the only document I could find was my Diners Club card. Since this had a number on it and attractive colours as well, it was taken to be important enough to be acceptable. Today was, so the police informed me, a national holiday and a feast was in progress. Anybody carrying such important documents as I displayed must be invited to the feast. Soon I found myself involved in eating wat and injara which might have tasted delicious had I not seen the vast quantities of flies covering every inch of this delectable dish. The meat tasted rotten and a maggot or two crawled out of several of the pieces. To swill this down a delicious mixture of brown vinegar was produced. The police delighted in pouring this vile liquid down their throats. Without doubt the meal at Itang was one of the most unpleasant that I have ever had to endure in any country in the world. At the time I wondered what Nuer food would be like and I consoled myself with the thought that however bad it turned out to be, it could not possibly be worse than what we were eating. Even Doereding disdained this particular feast.

When we tried to leave, the previously friendly attitude of the police changed. They pushed me toward a hut where a fat, dirty looking and more junior officer produced a torn exercise book with a few lines scribbled in it. This, I was told, was the official record book. We were to enter our names, then I would be allowed to proceed, but the officer wished to detain Doereding. I realized that something had gone wrong and decided it was time to bluff my way out of the mess otherwise we might be delayed for hours or even days. I drew from my pocket a letter of authority which the Ethiopian Government had provided in case of trouble. After the police lieutenant had ponderously read out aloud each line to his audience, he let us go.

For four or five hours we continued in the truck until eventually it ground to a halt with the back springs collapsing. The Indian driver cursed and declared that he would have to walk to Itang. We, on the other hand decided to abandon him and walk on in the opposite direction towards Teleuth, for already we had entered Nuer country. As we started our first hike I learnt the greeting which one exchanges with passing Nuer. "*Male,*" one would shout. "*Male m'gwa,*" would be the reply. "*Male m'edit,*" I would answer, and so on *ad infinitum*. Each elaboration of "*Male*" being a further greeting or reply. It was rather like passing an English acquaintance in the street shouting, "Hello". He would answer, "Hello you" and you would reply, "Hello you over there," until each of you got bored with the brisk repartee.

At first I found walking painful and exhausting, as did Doereding, who never ceased complaining that he was an old man unfit for this sort of thing. But gradually I got used to covering fairly long distances on foot. It seemed a good way to see the Nuer. Once or twice we came across small groups of tribesmen who expressed interest in me. Sometimes children dashed up without embarrassment grabbing at the hair on my arms and legs whilst shrieking with delight. To them, of course, a hairy European was a sort of monster from the wilds since in this part of Africa the tribes have no hair on their bodies and very little on their heads. The men do not need to shave and the few hairs that do appear are usually plucked out by hand. To them therefore my appearance must have been both 'aweful' and alarming, whilst they never recovered from the amusement of watching the way a European swings his arms. Most African peoples walk keeping their arms to their sides or slightly behind in order to conserve energy. The children would run along behind me swinging their arms in imitation. Indeed so many people now seemed to be joining us that my progression across Nuer land was already becoming somewhat similar to that of the Pied Piper. A lot of Nuer rough guys joined us merely for the enjoyment of hurling insults. Every once in a while Doereding would take a swipe at some of these with his broken umbrella.

As the sun set I began to wonder how and where we would spend our first night. I was worried about the fate of my medicine box and cameras which had been entrusted to a couple of Nuer who kept disappearing into the bush for long periods. Here again Doereding told me to set my mind at rest. "All will come right in the end," he explained with pride, "we are now amongst Nuer of the eastern clans and will be well treated".

When we stopped outside our first Nuer village I found that Doereding was well known to the girls. A small child with a high fever was brought and I gave it some penicillin. As soon as medicines were seen, an argument began and I was alarmed to discover that I was becoming the subject of an auction. Three important looking Nuer from different villages were fighting for the privilege of entertaining the foreigner. As Doereding explained, the main difficulty would be in deciding which village to select for the night. Ideally, in order to offend no one Doereding suggested that a third of the night should be spent in each village. I pointed out, somewhat illogically to his way of thinking, that I wanted to sleep. So we selected the village of the most powerful man in the area and settled down for the night amidst the burning of cow dung, the lowing of the cattle, the humming of mosquitoes and the endless high-pitched chatter of the Nuer. It seems as though when they meet there are always urgent matters to discuss. Most of the conversations taking place related, so I was told, to the activities of the rebels. Doereding, I thought, must have very close connections with the freedom fighters for everywhere the leaders of the people came to him to obtain the latest information of what was going on in South Sudan.

For the next few days we progressed across country in a similar fashion stopping at villages, treating the sick and receiving food and beer wherever we rested. Only once or twice did hostile Nuer, brandishing their spears, chase us away. Always as one entered a village collections of evil-looking mongrel dogs snapped and snarled. To protect one's ankles and legs it was necessary to carry a long stick; indeed when entering a village it was customary to swipe out right and left, occasionally catching one of the mongrel curs a good whack sending it yelping off into the swamp. Initially this seemed pretty brutal treatment, but with rabies rampant in the area it is not wise to take chances. Most of the dogs seemed to enjoy attacking visitors. They are probably encouraged to bark to frighten off enemies, especially at night. However, once you have passed into the circle of the village the dogs generally leave you alone. Outside the village they are incredibly unintelligent animals in that they never recognize anyone and will try to bite both friend and foe.

By the end of the second day Doereding and I formed a plan of action. We decided that we would head for the village of Gwal Diok, whose chief was Gar Quot, the head of the local court of justice. (The Nuer, one must remember do not have chiefs, as I shall explain in Chapter 4, but for simplicity's sake I shall refer to Gar Quot as a 'chief', since he was the person with the most authority in the village. In the event of any trouble in the area Gar Quot would have to account for it to the Ethiopian police.) His village was situated nearby the village of Wiu, the god of the sacred spear, and he was reputed to be a man of great strength. This Nuer chieftain, Gar Quot, had sent a message saying that I should come to his village but I did not really know quite why we were going there instead of going to Wiu itself. Doereding said that it would be better if we stayed outside the village of the prophet and also that Gar Quot would be offended if I refused his invitation. Nevertheless it is one thing for a Nuer chief to invite you to stay and quite another for him to arrange the reception of his visitors.

Gwal Diok could be seen from some distance because of the enormous crab apple tree growing in the centre of the village, which consisted of fifty to sixty inhabitants. Nuer villages are often strung together in one huge long line with sometimes only a few hundred yards separating them. To the foreigner, finding a particular village presents a considerable problem, especially at night, when one must remember that landing up unexpectedly in the wrong place could result in being shot as an enemy. Normally these lines of villages stretch out parallel on either side of large plains or swamps, the theory being that the cattle can then graze undisturbed in the centre, protected on either side by the tribesmen.

Gar Quot had been busy trying to organize a hut for us to live in. When we arrived at Gwal Diok we ran into an immediate difficulty, for all three of his wives refused to move out of their separate residences for an unwanted foreigner! These would have been the most suitable houses since they were near the chief's in the centre of the village. There was a lot of cursing from Gar Quot's wives whilst he chased them around with a stick threatening to beat them. The cattle charged about adding to the chaos, thoroughly alarmed by the commotion.

The sun was still directly overhead and there was no shade except under the main tree. Doereding and I let Gar Quot fight it out with his respective spouses and went to relax in the shade. Two hours later Gar Quot proudly announced that a house had been prepared. When we went to inspect this choice residence one glance told us that this 'house' had not been lived in for sometime; it had probably been used for storing grain or for harbouring sick cattle, possibly both. It smelt foul and the floor was filthy with cattle droppings. Doereding looked to the sky, then turned to Gar Quot and informed him that if this was the best that could be done, then we would seek refuge in another village where doubtless the chief would be able to offer appropriate hospitality. Gar Quot stunned by this rebuff decided that his loss of face would be too great if I were to go elsewhere. So as a last attempt he turned to Nyathiang, a distant relation of his whose husband happened to be away at that moment, and, picking her up by the scruff of the neck and seat of her leather skirt, hurled her plus most of her possessions out of her hut. I felt miserable at seeing the poor woman so treated on my account, but Doereding assured me that we could compensate her later; meanwhile we would hurt the feelings of the entire village if we failed to accept the new hut which Gar Quot was now offering.

At this stage I now noticed a small boy aged about 14 with wide tribal marks on his head, who stood close by. Indeed this silent observer was to be practically my ghost for the next fortnight. Wherever I went he was to follow meekly and quietly. Whenever help was needed he was sure to be there to assist without being asked. Always he would stand without making any noise or appearing to want recognition. Doereding concluded that he was a mentally retarded half wit. Kiir, for this was his name, started to clear out the hut for us and arranged for water to be brought from the Baro river 3 miles away. He rushed around attempting to block one or two mysterious looking holes in the side of the hut, which I learned later marked the comings and goings of rats which we had temporarily replaced.

Kiir had many qualities which were to endear him to me, not least of which was his willingness at all times to help in the preparation of meals. This was a delicate matter, for food in the Nuer country is normally prepared by a woman. Thus, having no wife or girlfriend amongst these people, I became dependent on either receiving someone else's food or on finding some male friend who was willing to cook for me in secret. Most men are ashamed to be seen bending over a cooking pot, except when they are at cattle camps with no women present. Kiir would sneak off when all was quiet and behind a screen of straw would make a small fire and start cooking. Only once did I reprimand Kiir and that was when on a certain occasion I caught sight of his hands. He had just been employed by his father in gathering up the still warm cow dung to make piles which would later be used for fires when the dung dried out. These cattle dung fires burn slowly letting off vast quantities of smoke which keep the mosquitoes away from both cattle and the village. Kiir's hands, still bore evidence of this occupation when he came to cook some delicious dish for my evening meal. When I complained about such a state of uncleanliness, he slunk off miserably and I, in turn, felt ashamed at having ticked him off in such a tactless manner.

Some days later at a dance I was to turn round and find Kiir standing behind me beneath a tree watching every motion but not daring himself to join in. I remember grabbing him by the hand and bringing him into the middle of what can only be described as chaos, whilst I watched the delight on his face at being included in this village festival. I never understood why Kiir was *persona non grata* with the village—not that they actively persecuted him, he was merely left out of everything. No one seemed to mind his attaching himself to me. Perhaps it was a relief for his family to know that he had something to do during the day. At night he would wait until he was sure I was ready to go to sleep, then he would silently disappear into the darkness. He seemed to have no friends, no one asked him to join their fishing parties or to sit with them around the camp fire. From the moment I first met him to the moment when I left Nuer country, he hardly uttered a word. Even to Doereding Kiir was a complete mystery, and once he had dismissed him as a mental defective he never thought to offer him food or drink. Perhaps Kiir had cried out from fear at the terrible moment of his initiation ceremony of garring or perhaps he really was mentally defective, I shall never know.

Settling in at Gwal Diok

CHAPTER 4

> The people are moving here because of the discomfort of war. . . .
> You will be driven across the village . . . so as to become a guest.

There are certain things that one can and cannot do when living amongst the Nuer. It was up to Doereding to keep me constantly on the right path. Since he spoke quite good English this should have been an easy task but my difficulties generally arose during Doereding's frequent absences. For him it was almost impossible to resist the attractions of a pretty girl and just when I needed him most to help with some impossible situation he would disappear and no one with the best will in the world would be able to find him. Either he would be drinking aragy (distilled corn wine) with a newly found relation or he would be attempting to open negotiations with the parents of an attractive maiden—a small fee would often secure the favours of the girl for one night. Sometimes he skipped the formalities and simply went chasing across the fields following a screaming female. His complaint to me on the outward journey that he was an old man seemed to have been forgotten!

The women found it more difficult to get used to the foreigner who had landed in their midst. To begin with it was the children who made the first approach to me and came to inspect the hairy monster. Then the mothers arrived to retrieve their offspring. I found that any false move on my part would send everybody running away terrified. The only solution was to remain seated occasionally playing my tape recorder and in this way I found it easy to fascinate the women and children. To hear their own voices must have been something as amazing to them as men landing on the moon was at first to us in Western civilization. My morning shave also drew the crowds, but to be fair they mostly came in the hope of receiving free medicine, as 'sick parade' always followed shaving.

It was during one of Doereding's lengthy disappearing acts that I found myself in Gwal Diok and suddenly received a call of nature. This was particularly embarrassing as the Nuer train themselves to exercise the functions of nature during the night when they cannot be seen. It is a cardinal sin to be spotted squatting anywhere on the plain, though absolutely permissable to urinate in public. As there are few trees and the villages tend to overlook each other, a serious call of nature in daylight may require a lengthy hike. Should this be caused by a case of mild dysentery or stomach disorder the situation may become desperate. I could never solve the problem but I can certainly guarantee that I have never seen a Nuer caught unawares, whereas, alas, I was constantly getting into trouble.

In my case it was perhaps more difficult because wherever I went I tended to be followed by a large crowd. In the early days it was the children but as I got to know the villages around Gwal Diok, the men would often come with me hoping something exciting was going to happen or at least that they would be able to present me to their friends. On this occasion I was in a fairly desperate state so I set out swiftly across the plains in the boiling heat of the sun. A large black sombrero, purchased in London's Carnaby Street, kept away the worst of the sun's rays. Beneath this an old khaki shirt and a pair of torn shorts protected part of my body, whilst Hush Puppies remained firmly glued to my feet. Grasping a stick which Kiir had given me as protection against the dogs I set off to find a suitably quiet spot.

After what was in fact a 4 to 5 mile hike I found myself alone at last and settled down comfortably beneath an isolated tree. All was well; no Nuer were about but at just that moment I was to find that the marshlands provide unexpected surprises. As I looked upwards a large brown cobra was gazing down at my sombrero. The distance could not have been more than a few feet and the snake appeared to be in an excellent position for pouncing. I could think of no method of beating a hasty retreat. And so we squatted there, the cobra and I, looking at each other with dismay. Guardedly, with a crab like movement I managed to retreat around the tree to the far side. Only then did I realize that I had been squatting over a hole in the ground which undoubtedly was the snake's home. He would have been fully justified in striking at me with all his hatred and venom (in all senses of the word), but perhaps the situation was so disastrous that the cobra was as stunned as I was.

Somewhat shaken I headed back for Gwal Diok only to find that it is not always easy to locate one's own village amongst a string of Nuer dwellings stretched across the horizon. True, Gwal Diok had one large tree in its midst which made it simpler to distinguish than many others, but in spite of this landmark it took me some time to find my way home in the increasingly oppressive heat. I vowed never again to go on a hike like this without a water bottle, for my thirst had become almost overwhelming.

Doereding and I tried to make our house as comfortable as possible. Besides storing water and food we managed to find goatskins to lie and sit upon, whilst I erected a totem pole outside. Nearly every Nuer house has some form of shrine—normally an altar to the spirits. If someone had been killed by lightning, sticks are twisted into special shapes and planted in the ground. Frequently when sacrifices are made small pieces of the animal are tied to these sticks. On my totem pole the British flag in the form of a cap was to fly with a certain bravado that might have been reminiscent of former days of the Empire.

One or two helpers were required to make life more tolerable for a foreigner like myself. Kiir was always there, but although he was reasonably helpful he did not command the necessary attention or respect to get things done. So I looked around, hoping

Gwal Diok. (*below*) Cattle dung burns to keep off mosquitoes

(*left*) Kiir, the author's faithful admirer

(*right*) Thiwat wearing his hat

to spot some youth with both position and the necessary strength to carry my heavy film equipment. One day as I was sitting under the big tree in the village and watching the girls smoking their long pipes, I spotted a boy called Thiwat who had a certain presence about him. Thiwat was no beauty, but he had a constant grin on his face; around his neck attached to a piece of leather he wore two leopard teeth. Small metal earrings were sometimes inserted in his pierced ears, these being frequently worn by Nuer warriors. When he sat with the elders under the village tree they paid attention to what Thiwat said. This was probably because Gar Quot had married his mother, who in turn had first been married to Gar Quot's brother before he died. The Nuer have adopted the habit of marrying their brother's widow in the event of his death, as it is essential not to leave a widow to fend for herself. If there are several brothers remaining the elder brother will accept the added responsibility, particularly if the girl is attractive or a hard worker. The Nuer claim that this is not a true marriage but rather an 'automatic adoption'.

Later on that day I saw Thiwat participating in a strange ceremony. The villagers were clustered around Nyathiang's other house in a semi-circle. (It will be remembered Gar Quot had thrown her out of one house in order to accommodate us.) They began by chanting prayers in their high-pitched voices. First there would be a scream from the leader of the chorus, then the rest would join in muttering invocations to the spirits. Nyathiang was the centre of attraction; on the ground in front of her there was a gourd, a small leopard skin, a series of cowrie shells, a couple of fly whisks and a tethered goat. Elsewhere the rest of the village were carrying on their normal tasks of mending the roofs or, in the case of women, pounding grain. Those involved in what was to become of Nyathiang's sacrifice took the whole business rather half heartedly, some even joking and laughing in the middle of their prayers. Partially concealed behind a tree, I watched this strange Nuer ceremony, (through the lens of my camera), hardly believing that it could be taking place in this modern age. My tape recorder was also in action picking up the sounds of the villagers and in particular Nyathiang's agonizing groans as she became gradually possessed by one of the Spirits of the Above, Kuoth Nhial.

After suitable invocations and libations, Nyathiang rose to her feet and clasping the shrine outside her hut swayed backwards and forwards, her voice gradually changing to that of a man. This was the same phenomenon I had witnessed on the first visit to the Nuer, when I was present at a similar ceremony. Nyathiang lurched around the area of her hut swaying violently in a movement which supposedly indicated that the spirits were searching for something or someone. Suddenly she grabbed a spear and taking the goat by the head, swiftly slit its throat. It was amazing that anyone in such a trance could have sufficient control over their movements, for it was only when the sacrifice had been completed that she sank back to the ground seemingly exhausted.

Then she was rubbed with butter and pieces of goat were placed on her stomach; other bits were attached to the shrine outside her hut. A small leopard skin was hung around her neck, whilst the prayers continued amongst the assembled company. Later I discovered that this had been a sacrifice to Deng, god of fertility—for Nyathiang had never produced a child.

Evans-Pritchard said in his book on Nuer religion that sacrifices are never performed by Nuer women, but no one seemed to regard Nyathiang's sacrifice as anything out of the ordinary. She was in fact considered to be a hereditary local priestess (of which there are many amongst the Nuer) and had the power to perform sacrifices for other people; this one, however, had been entirely for her own benefit. Thiwat who had been present all the time explained the reason for her barren state. In her childhood she had found a stone in the swamps which must have been a representation of the spirit Biel. She should have left the stone alone, but instead, being captivated by its beauty she picked it up and took it home. Her barrenness was attributed to the possession of this stone. Later in life when things started to go wrong Nyathiang had hurled the stone into the river, but the bad luck had remained.

After the sacrifice Thiwat came to my hut and, with Doereding acting as interpreter, I asked him if he would work with me for a wage. This was refused as being undignified. Gar Quot, he claimed, needed him to look after the cattle. When I suggested that he might appear in a cine film that I was making for television, he was so embarrassed at the idea of cameras looking at him or into his soul, that he again refused. There was no method of winning over Thiwat without Gar Quot's approval. So I consulted the chief, who not only agreed that Thiwat should help me but even insisted that he should become my official guide and interpreter. Nominated in this manner Thiwat was able to regard his duty with pride. From somewhere in his hut he produced an extraordinary article of clothing which he wore constantly in my presence. It was his only garment and turned out to be a much battered straw hat! Somehow as he stood naked, silhouetted against the skyline, there seemed something rather incongruous about this splendid native figure of a man retaining, perched on his head, a derelict representation of European culture. We frequently travelled across country together, Thiwat with his hat, Doereding with his broken umbrella, two spokes sticking into the air, Kiir covered in cow dung and myself with cameras slung around me like a Christmas tree. We must have presented a strange sight to the Nuer!

I soon discovered that the tribesmen were seldom willing to help carry one's burdens. A Nuer friend of mine when visiting London once told me that the worst thing about England was that he was expected to carry his girl friend's suitcase. Nuer men never carry anything if possible other than a spear, all burdens being borne by the women. Even when they are willing to help, the men are often physically incapable of carrying heavy burdens over long distances, arm and leg muscles being underdeveloped compared with Europeans. Occasionally Thiwat would stagger along with my cine camera, but soon he would find himself becoming so exhausted that I would be obliged to take over the burden myself. On the other hand, my light aluminium tripod was just the sort of thing that the Nuer enjoyed carrying: that is if they had to carry anything at all. It was light. It was easy to put on the shoulder and it might even be mistaken for some strange type of weapon e.g. maching gun or mortar. In other words, the tripod became a status symbol and was therefore acceptable. Of course there are occasions when men have to carry burdens over long distances, but these are probably rare.

The final key to my acceptance in Gwal Diok lay with Gar Quot and Doereding. It was essential that these two should get on together and it was with some relief that I noticed that they were becoming great friends. Equally I was lucky that they both appeared to like me. Gar Quot can only be described as a man of enormous proportions. The Nuer are tall, many of them reaching 6 foot and above, and they look even taller because of their nakedness. Gar Quot must have approached 7 foot and was a giant amongst the tribe. Everything about him was large. He carried a huge aluminium stick with a spike on the end as a badge of office and was the only Nuer I came across to be, on occasion, properly dressed in a blue shirt and corduroy trousers. This was saved for special events, for normally he would be found wandering around the village wearing no clothes, shouting orders and unsuccessfully attempting to organize everyone.

The Nuer have no official chiefs, as I have already stated, nor indeed have they ever had them. The religious prophets of the gods, Kiir, Deng and Wiu are, in my view, the real leaders. (See Chapter 7). There are also a number of other officials some of them hereditary, such as the 'men of cattle' and the 'leopard skin priests' who, in the olden days, commanded a degree of respect. At first it was the British district commissioners in South Sudan, and later their Sudanese successors who tried to instigate a form of chieftain authority in order to replace the spiritual leaders who had taken a stand against the government. So some senior citizen who was thought to be strong or brave was selected to be the representative village chief and would be held responsible for the good conduct of his people. Should the village go on raids or become involved in disputes requiring police intervention, then the 'chief' would be expected to produce the criminals or provide the government with a fine of cattle. This unenviable task made most 'chiefs' unpopular and they themselves were reluctant to assume the responsibility.

Automatic equality exists amongst the Nuer, since there is no class system. Even Gar Quot had to get things done by putting a reasoned argument to his people. Indeed, Gar Quot's power must also have been due to his powerful personality, since some of his people were from different clans of the eastern Nuer who had been expelled from the Sudan. Somehow the Ethiopian police had managed to persuade Gar Quot to be in charge of the entire area. Not only was he responsible for Gwal Diok but also for some forty to fifty other villages containing perhaps five thousand inhabitants in all.

The characteristic expression of the Nuer was cheerful and smiling, like Thiwat's. By contrast Gar Quot was often scowling. Two large buck teeth protuded over his lower lip. His voice was like the bellow of an angry bull and could be heard a mile away. But there were times when he would sit peacefully under the tree in Gwal Diok, humming ancient songs and accompanying himself on the Nuer tom—a string instrument of great antiquity.

Ever since my arrival in Gwal Diok, Gar Quot had been anxious to impress me with his authority. The accommodation arrangements had not been too successful, much to his embarrassment, so by way of compensation he offered to present me with a ram belonging to his brother. Not unnaturally the brother refused to co-operate, and it was not until Gar Quot had given him several cuffs about the ears that he went off to fetch the scraggiest ram he possessed. As soon as the beast had been produced and tethered outside my hut, Gar Quot advised me to kill and eat it immediately. At first I could not understand his anxiety since now it was my ram, in my possession, and as I was in no hurry for food, I foolishly delayed killing it. During the night the ram was stolen and for the next few days the farce continued. No sooner was the ram found by Gar Quot and placed outside my hut, than it would disappear again to be hidden away in another village. So infuriated did Gar Quot become with this challenge to his authority, that eventually he killed the ram himself and ordered me to eat every piece of the meat before his very eyes. When I wanted to share this delicacy with Doereding, Thiwat and Kiir, Gar Quot tried to stop me. The meat was not consumed raw but was half-cooked first by Kiir over the fire. As only small bits of meat can be dealt with at any one time, they were left on the side for a while, where swarms of flies settled on the flesh. Some time later these titbits were produced as a delicacy with the flies still swarming about them. In Nuer country flies are flies and something one just has to get used to! As I sat eating my ram, for the first time I was beginning to feel 'settled in' at Gwal Diok, though somewhat fearful of dysentery. At least, it appeared, I was achieving a degree of acceptance which had been missing on my previous trip.

Sick Parade

CHAPTER 5

Spirits Above you promised to support us.
We have fought well and sacrificed an animal.
Yet why do we find illness amongst our people?

One easy method of becoming accepted by a primitive people is through medicine. Frequently I have made initial contact by treating a sick child, or bringing relief to someone in agony. I have never taken a medical degree or indeed any instruction in the administration of medicine. Nor originally could I claim to have possessed much medical knowledge other than that gained by reading a small pocket booklet (originally recommended by the Royal Geographical Society to its Fellows) entitled the *Explorer's Guide to Medicine*. This admirable volume was issued as a sort of handbook of tropical diseases but it had decided drawbacks. Firstly some of the descriptions are so limited that the reader can barely understand the description of the symptons let alone the cures. Secondly, a frequent suggestion in the *Explorer's Guide* is that the patient should be taken to the nearest hospital —quite impracticable in most cases. The other source of irritation is that the writer appears to have been trained in somewhat brutal military medicine—the recommended cure often being "administer per rectum". Finally the *Explorer's Guide* failed to mention many of the antibiotics which had been given me by the hospitals in London, as these were recent inventions.

I had travelled out with a vast quantity of triplopen—three types of penicillin in one. This was prepared in powder form so that it could be mixed fairly swiftly with distilled water. As I did not want to rely on being able to find any water, let alone distilled, I brought a vast quantity of small capsules which could be broken open and mixed with the penicillin powder. Having heard of the difficulties of sterilizing medical implements, I decided to take a number of needles which could be used on one occasion only and then discarded. When it came to syringes, the ideal solution would have been to carry several hundred, but as these were both bulky and expensive, I limited myself to a dozen taking a chance on using the same syringe for a number of patients. In giving intramuscular injections this is not as dangerous as it may sound.

In London I needed to practice giving a swift jab home, rather like playing darts, in order to send a quivering needle deep into the upper part of an unsuspecting backside. The difficulty was to find the opportunity. My friends and particularly my housekeeper, were unwilling to offer themselves as targets. It was only when a doctor suggested that a squash ball had about the same consistency as African skin that I could practice the art of giving injections. The same doctor suggested one other refinement. It was thought that in order to be completely sanitary I should have a vast number of pairs of plastic gloves. These articles could be swiftly torn off a piece of paper, used and then discarded. Needless to say my patients thought them ridiculous. Some of the women squealed when touched by them, so that eventually I had to throw away all my plastic gloves. Penicillin was to be my main cure, and since most of the tribes had developed no resistance as yet, there was little danger in its administration. Few diseases are likely to be made worse by penicillin and therefore I believe it to be a fairly safe treatment.

Obviously a variety of drugs would be needed to combat the diseases which I knew would be prevalent in the area. In London therefore, I had equipped myself with various types of eye ointments, disinfectant powders, anti-dysentery pills, anti-malaria tablets, bandages and a number of specialized drugs with which I was hoping to experiment. Admittedly this all sounds rather hit and miss medicine, but when you remember that I was to be in an area where there was literally no other medical aid, it is perhaps possible to forgive this somewhat amateur approach. I always apply a number of golden rules which have stood me in good stead throughout Africa. The first is not to become conceited and think I can cure everything just because there have been a number of lucky occasions when something has worked out well. Without medical training it is absurd to attempt to cure the seriously ill or dying. Indeed in Africa it is dangerous to do so, for should a patient die the relatives may well suggest that it was the fault of the white man. The mere presence of a white man at the time of death may be thought to be an unlucky omen. Again, this may sound heartless, but it has often meant that I have been able to operate successfully in an area where a recognized doctor who had taken the Hippocratic oath would have been at a decided disadvantage. A qualified doctor would have felt it his or her duty to treat all patients, especially those who were on the point of death, in an attempt to save them, no matter what the odds against recovery. In wilder parts it is no good explaining afterwards that the patient would have died anyway. Such logic would often be unacceptable to the distressed relatives of the deceased.

To give but one example of the callousness which I found it necessary to adopt. On my second night in Gwal Diok, I was woken and urged to come quickly to the assistance of a man who was ill in a nearby village. Doereding refused to move when Thiwat, interrupting our slumbers, told us that "we must come quickly". At about four o'clock in the morning therefore Thiwat and I set out together for the next village. This turned out to be 5 miles away (not just a few minutes walk as we had been lead to believe) so that by the time we got there I was not in a particularly good mood. No sooner had we entered the village, beating off the howling dogs as usual, than I was led to the hut of a man who was truly dying. It needed only a glance to see that there was no possibility of saving the miserable heap of skin and bones lying on the floor of the darkened hut. I have seldom seen a living skeleton but such was the case before me. There was no flesh anywhere on the man's body, so that even an injection seemed impossible. He was said not to have eaten anything for a week and his breathing was of that heavy type normally associated with death. His colour suggested that he was dying from some form of hepatitis or jaundice—which was prevalent, sometimes being caused, I would guess, by the urine of rats which rummaged amongst the grain and left the seeds of disease behind them. Experienced medical opinions may well disprove this theory, but I hold to the belief that rats are responsible for jaundice in this area. I held up my hands in resignation trying to explain to the relatives of the dying man that there was nothing I could do.

As dawn began to appear Thiwat and I made our way back to Gwal Diok. I felt depressed by my ineffectiveness. I could bring no comfort to this dying man, and it did not help to know that even had he been on the door-steps of one of our best teaching hospitals in England, it would still have been too late for him to be saved. Above all I was determined not to be one of those people who pretend to bring aid by giving the tribesmen a few aspirin. Perhaps, had he been conscious, I might have produced some pills, something out of sheer pity and therefore been culpable, as well as endangering myself.

At sunrise the village was astir and cattle were churning up the dust as they headed off to seek grazing. I had returned to my hut but abandoned the idea of trying to make up for lost sleep. At this time of day I found I often wanted to sit alone and think. There is so little privacy when living a tribal existence and that morning I felt reluctant to enter into daily activity. I was more irritable than usual when, after a mere half an hour's rest, I was presented with some hundred patients suffering from countless different diseases. I was still feeling exhausted from lack of sleep and in no mood to see any more cases of misery, yet I could not disappoint people who might have come many miles in search of a cure.

It is perhaps worthwhile to digress at this stage to explain that there are few medical centres in the Southern Sudan or Western Ethiopia outside the towns. The distances involved are not so great that under normal conditions people who are seriously ill could not be brought to the towns, but the political situation (as explained in the appendices) is such that crossing the swamps and marshes can be extremely dangerous. The tribesmen dislike travelling alone when there is the danger of either being attacked by other tribes or being shot by the Sudanese army or the rebels. Often the traveller cannot win: if he is not shot, he will be robbed, beaten up or perhaps even captured and taken away into so-called slavery. It is not therefore surprising that most of the sick prefer to remain in the relative safety of their villages in the hope of being cured by nature rather than run the risk of almost certain death by travelling abroad. When I arrived amongst the Nuer the word soon went round that a white man who was living in Gwal Diok could effect cures. There was no difficulty in finding patients—for the Nuer have few cures themselves other than by sacrifices—the danger was that the whole area, and particularly my village, would be swamped with them.

This morning's batch brought the usual problems. A child lay in its mother's arms hidden by a piece of cloth and sucking at her breast. As it was presented to me I saw the terrible signs of inherited syphilis—two huge holes had bored into the head, one on the temple and the other on the cheek, looking just as though the poor infant had been shot with two bullets. A number of limping men and women stood around with wounds covered by mud and reeds—these were suffering from yaws and were certainly undergoing considerable pain. Malaria was taking its toll. My only difficulty was to decide whether or not to try to effect a cure or to let it burn itself out—since the native inhabitants had obviously developed their own resistance levels. Tracoma is well known throughout Africa and the Nuer suffer as badly from this as many other tribes. As usual there were a vast number of people sitting around with badly infected eyes covered with flies. Some old man coughed, spitting blood on the ground:

some of the cattle in the village must be tubercular, I concluded. Doereding claimed that once a government official had tested the cattle for tuberculosis and suggested removing the diseased animals. The thought had been so preposterous to the Nuer, to whom cattle represent wealth, that the official had been lucky to escape with his life. I had been warned to try nothing so foolish.

I found that Gwal Diok besides suffering from the normal diseases was going through a mild epidemic of whooping cough. I would also estimate that something like 20 per cent of the population of the village was suffering from TB and another 10 per cent from dysentery. The few people suffering from syphilis were giving it to others, but I was happy to have caught one or two women with yaws at an early stage, before they had been able to infect the entire area. The dysentery came mostly as a result of the women drawing water from a local pond rather than walking 3 miles to the Baro river for fresh water. I tried to explain to Gar Quot that he must make the villagers go to the river for their water supplies unless he wanted the whole village to be sick.

One good-looking young man of about 20 appeared with a foot roughly treble the normal size. He had been fishing. The mud fish carry a particular poison in the spikes of their spine which can be extremely dangerous. A number of Nuer die from such infections and the warrior before me was obviously frightened as well as in extreme pain. I decided to take a chance and give him an injection of a million units of triplopen. It turned out that this was to be one of my most successful patients, for two days later he came to me with his foot completely cured, an enormous grin on his face. In his opinion the cure had been so miraculous that, much to my dismay, throughout my visit this disciple never ceased recommending me to his friends. Moreover, as he explained to the crowds gathering around him how he had received an injection from the white man, I found it increasingly difficult to convince other patients that on some occasions pills could be equally effective. Everyone started by demanding injections and often it became impossible to discover what was wrong with the patients who came to the sick parades. They would prepare themselves by lying on the ground, buttocks upwards. Old ladies would shake with rage when they failed to 'receive the needle'. Men would threaten me with spears. Frequently people came simply because they were old and hoped that by some miracle the white man might be able to restore their youth.

If one of the greatest difficulties was to discover the symptoms or obtain from the sick a description of their pains, the other drawback was my inability to get any form of organization into the sick parades. Firstly, I had somehow to explain that I could not be treating people all day long. Therefore I set aside two or three hours in the early morning for treatment of diseases. Obviously this strict rule had frequently to be broken, since accidents tend to occur at almost any time of the day or night. For instance when on one occasion a warrior stood before me with a spear through his leg, I could hardly explain to him that he should present himself at sick parade next morning. In that case I stopped filming, attempted to hack off the end of the spear without simultaneously taking away part of the man's leg, stemmed the flow of blood, disinfected the wound in so far as possible and finally applied my usual cure of a good stiff penicillin injection. Amazingly enough the man and his leg survived! This was probably more of a tribute to his powers of endurance and recuperation than to my skill.

Apart from the difficulty of gathering people together at a specific time to treat them, there was the problem of having insufficient supplies of particular medicines. My eye ointments ran out after the first week. So somewhat pathetically, day after day, I had to turn away hundreds suffering from eye diseases with the explanation that I had no more medicine. A small tube of eye ointment in this area carried such value that it could easily be sold to the tribesmen for $3 Ethiopian, roughly ten times what it should cost. My own policy is always to give medicine and not to charge for it, but most of the missionaries anywhere near this area charged for medicine to support their other worthwhile activities such as the conversion of souls to Christianity. I still find their arguments somewhat puzzling, nor can I quite agree that it is necessary to charge the natives in order to make them appreciate the aid one is bringing. This business of charging for medicine had indeed done considerable harm. A few Nuer trained previously by the British in hospitals, now travel amongst the tribes pretending to be modern doctors. One or two of them keep an old syringe and a needle, and for enormous sums of money attempt to give injections. Since the syringes contain sand, their needles are old and rusty and the drugs they use are probably out of date, it is amazing that they do not kill everyone they touch.

Doereding never ceased fretting over the fact that my medicine was free, for he dreamt of the possibilities of selling it to his people—and by local standards becoming a millionaire in the process. Doubtless he still blames me for thwarting his ambitions.

In an attempt to organize the sick parades I got Doereding to divide the people into groups of diseases. I wanted all the eye patients on one side, all those suffering from dysentery on the other and so forth; little did I realize that this totally disregarded Nuer laws of precedence. These require that people should be treated in turn as they arrive, except for local men of power who should have the privilege of queue barging because of their position. Basically, also, men should take precedence over women and children, although I have known some Nuer men suffering quite badly themselves to bring foward their children for treatment before mentioning their own ailments. Today, every time Doereding succeeded in getting one group together, someone amongst the 'eyes' would see a friend standing amongst the 'dysentery' and the two would rush to greet each other.

It was important that my patients should not move about between diagnosis and treatment for it was almost impossible for me to tell the difference between a number of the Nuer. In their turn they must have thought me extremely stupid, not being able to remember for two seconds running what they had just told me about their symptoms and diseases. The fact that they had moved from the left-hand side of the group to the far right appeared to them irrelevant—I was expected to recognize them wherever they were, since they could so easily recognize me!

There was also a continual tendency to close in on my hut, for I could not get Doereding to force people to stand or sit at a distance, to give us breathing space. I was not particularly keen to have so many sick people literally on top of me. Doereding normally kept his temper and seemed to be amazingly patient with everyone, but sometimes he took the side of the Nuer against me, regarding any form of organization as 'white man's folly'. It was only when he realized that by organization we managed to get things done more swiftly that he was gradually won over to my strange ways.

Once when I was treating a man in an advanced stage of syphilis a fairly typical scene took place. Two old ladies rushed everywhere demanding immediate treatment and were obviously bent on causing havoc. Perhaps they thought the whole thing was a bit too serious and an element of frivolity should be introduced. Both old girls wanted an injection and prepared themselves for it by attempting to push aside the man whom I was treating and who was lying down in the ground in front of me. I told Doereding to deal with these troublesome females. This was evidently just what they had hoped would happen, for they hurled every form of abuse at poor Doereding, making fun of him and saying that unless he helped them he would not be welcome in their villages. One, whose daughter Doereding knew well, threatened, to the amusement of the crowd, to prevent him from seeing the girl in future. As Doereding advanced to push them back they flayed out at him with vigour so that, much to his discomfort, he had to retreat midst much laughter. The situation rapidly deteriorated. So I decided to down tools, announcing that unless order was restored I would cease treatment. In this way the crowd was won over and the old ladies were pulled out of the arena cursing and swearing. When the dust had settled I was able to start again with my line of patients lying or sitting on goat skins on the ground.

Just as 'the needle was about to be put away' in the phraseology of the Nuer, a procession could be seen approaching the village: a woman was being carried on a stretcher made of reeds. When the party arrived they laid the patient on the ground before me explaining that they had come a long distance out of the Sudan and into Ethiopia on hearing that a white doctor was in the area. Although I denied that I was a doctor, the evidence of so many patients surrounding me was taken to mean that I must be a medicine man. There was no excuse for not treating this woman. The rather attractive female lying on the stretcher was approximately 25 years of age. She had suffered a bad miscarriage and was still bleeding profusely. I rushed to the *Explorer's Guide* thumbing through the index, but, alas, miscarriage did not appear to be part of the explorer's training! Penicillin seemed the only hope, though I had not the slightest idea whether an injection would do any good. The womb also had to be cleansed. I was sure that having been carried all this way it was essential for me to do something. The woman and her party remained several hours outside my hut before setting off again for the Sudan. Meanwhile I had given some general instructions about stopping the flow of blood. To this day, however, I am uncertain of the fate of that poor girl, and wonder whether the journey was really worthwhile or whether she would not have had a better chance of survival by remaining quietly at home in her own village.

After treating a number of children and feeling somewhat relieved that at last most of the patients had now been dealt with, I took the final small girl aged about 7 on to my lap and began trying to diagnose her illness. Strange bumps erupted from under her skin—a high fever—irregular breathing and fast pulse. Doereding let out a yell moving backwards. The child sitting on my knee was suffering from smallpox! This was the first case of smallpox I had seen, although I was later to come across many more and to become slightly more careful as a result of this initial contact. I could do nothing but tell the mother to take her child back to their village and attempt to isolate the area. The prophet Kor Jum had already forbidden day dances from taking place where smallpox

A married Nuer girl in the rain

The fishing festival

was known to exist. Yet any attempt to keep nomadic pastoral peoples in one place by isolating areas is almost bound to fail. Therefore smallpox amongst the Nuer has already proved a disaster recently killing vast numbers of tribesmen. The same is true today of cholera, which has recently broken out in South Sudan.

I had had enough for one day—one man due to die of hepatitis, a bad miscarriage, and finally this young girl, for whom I could do nothing, suffering from smallpox and bound to spread it. There seemed only one thing to do. Retreat to my hut and make a cup of gaelic coffee; whisky was in my flask and cream was not hard to come by.

A Fishing Party

CHAPTER 6

Buk give us a fish
Buk give us a fish
Bless us whilst in the water
Keep us from danger
Mother of Deng, we pray for this.
(Fishing song to Buk.)

For some time now the young warriors had been waiting for the cattle camps to break up before returning home to their villages. The people I had met so far in Gwal Diok such as Gar Quot, Thiwat, Kiir, etc., were what might be termed 'the advance party' whose job it was to prepare for those who would be coming later. Many of the girls were waiting eagerly for the return of their boy friends. For four or five long months Nuer youths had been in virtual isolation with their cattle in the grazing grounds near the rivers. Now it was May; the rains would soon fall and there would be plenty of grazing for the cattle near the villages.

When the rains fall, the swamps fill up and mosquitoes increase and multiply—life becoming almost unbearable, even for the Nuer. In the cattle camps existence is always fairly rough with the men performing women's chores such as milking the cows and cooking their own food. Occasionally young women visit the camp to bring their loved ones small delicacies such as pieces of dried cattle blood baked and moulded into blocks. Or again, provided the distance is not too great, a group of girls might make some white beer and bring it in pumpkin gourds as a special treat. It was difficult for me to imagine what cattle camp life is really like, but the tribesmen told me they soon became bored with their isolation and longed for the time of their return. They can then drive their cattle towards the homesteads, and live in their villages again.

For several days Gar Quot had been talking about the return of his cattle. He explained to me that as soon as the rains came the Nuer would be very busy. More houses would be built, rope would be made, fishing festivals would take place, weddings, dances and the ceremonial garring or cutting of the heads, would all occur. I had become impatient for activity and wondered how all the new people, who were soon to arrive in Gwal Diok, would regard the foreigner they would find in their midst. On the one hand I wanted everyone to return so that I could get a more complete picture of Nuer life, but on the other I somewhat dreaded having to make new friends. Above all I wondered how the inhabitants of the house which I was occupying would react when they found me taking up valuable space and eating precious food. Although Nyathiang had, under duress from Gar Quot, lent me the use of her house, this would normally have been shared by a number of her relations in the cattle camp when they returned.

Nuer tend to sleep in vastly over-crowded conditions resting up against each other. It is not unusual for five or six people to lie crowded in a tiny hut. I was aware that I must be sleeping on someone else's goatskin and using someone else's large gourds for water. Still I hoped that those who were to return could be won over in the same way as had been the inhabitants of Gwal Diok whom I had already met. Perhaps they too could use the services of an unqualified medical practicioner, and would resign themselves to this uninvited guest.

One morning during the first week spent in Gwal Diok (and by then I must admit I had already begun to lose track of time), Thiwat woke me in the early hours to announce that we were going fishing. One of his main jobs as my protector and guardian seemed to be always to ensure that as soon as I was sound asleep, I should be woken up; but perhaps this is unkind for his intentions were sincere enough. I had seen several people of the village jabbing their spears into a small muddy pond a few hundred yards away and I imagined that Thiwat was inviting me to join in this seemingly useless pursuit. Doereding, however, explained that greater things were intended: it was proposed that we should go to meet the men coming back from the cattle camps. A fishing festival would then take place when hundreds of tribesmen would drive the mud fish from one end of the lake to the other. I suppose I should have been more cautious and tried to discover exactly where this lake was, but somewhat unwisely once again I accepted Thiwat's 'not very far' as being an adequate explanation of the distance involved. In fact, although we set out in the early hours of the morning we did not reach the lake until approximately two o'clock in the afternoon. This meant a hike during the worst heat of the day. Again somewhat unwisely Doereding and I departed without having taken a cooked breakfast or indeed any type of breakfast at all. Even more stupidly I had only half filled my water bottle so that by the time we finally arrived all our drinking water was gone.

I had been assured that the fishing festival would be a beautiful sight, and so Thiwat, Doereding and myself had set out with my Bolex 16mm camera, plus the Leica slung around my neck. After about a mile Thiwat announced that the Bolex case and film was too heavy, whilst Doereding, having tested the weight, confirmed that no Nuer could possibly be expected to carry anything like this. The result was that I swung the strap over my own shoulders and staggered forward assuring both companions that really the burden was extremely light! Thiwat wore his one and only European possession—the torn straw hat. Doereding carried his usual umbrella with the broken spokes, and I carried my blasted camera! We must indeed have looked a strange procession especially since we sported no visible weapons. Normally when any party attempts to cover such distances one or two body-guards carrying rifles accompany the group. Even if there is no ammunition, it is thought that the sight of the rifle slung over their shoulders is likely to be a sufficient deterrent to any enemy. Attached to my belt was an army revolver which John Blower had lent me. I tried to assure Thiwat and Doereding that although this could not be seen from afar, it was equally effective. I only hoped I would never have to use it, for although I quite fancy myself as a revolver shot when aiming at stationary tin cans, placed at distance no greater than 10 yards away, I would hesitate to guarantee getting anywhere near a moving target.

As noon approached and it grew hotter, I began to find my energy flagging. From time to time Thiwat, who was leading, would look around and fret at the slowness of our progress. Doereding never believed in rushing, and in my case the weight of the Bolex caused me to stumble over the rough ground. This should have been an ideal opportunity to admire the beauty of the countryside—the vast swamps and the multi-coloured birds—but I could only think of the journey's end repeatedly asking how much further we had to go. Thiwat would always answer 'not far', but even Doereding was becoming irritated by this reply. There were moments when I thought Thiwat did not know where he was leading us. Since most of the tribesmen we passed *en route* were Anuak there was no point in asking directions from them. The Anuak, normally being enemies of the Nuer, were hardly likely to offer us worthwhile advice or assistance.

When we came to a part of the Baro river which had to be crossed Thiwat and Doereding started ahead, walking gingerly and balancing their bundles of clothes on their heads. I stood on the bank realizing that I could not possibly carry clothes and cameras on my head whilst maintaining my balance against the strong current. Twice I tried and nearly fell over. Just as I was beginning to lose my temper, I spotted an Anuak canoe a few hundred yards downstream. With great luck I managed to find the owner and was on the point of striking a bargain with him to take me across the river, when Thiwat and Doereding reappeared having returned to help me. As soon as the Anuak saw that I was with Nuer, there was no price at which he would take me across the river; he went off spitting on the ground and muttering curses. Of course I could have taken the canoe without permission, but this might well have started a fight and would have been extremely dangerous. It was not the sort of thing you do in this area, for a canoe is a valuable asset, not to be borrowed without its owner's consent.

Once again we got ready to cross on our own, this time with Thiwat taking my Bolex on his head while Doereding handed me a heavy stick to help me keep my balance against the current. It was a considerable feat to cross that river. At times the water was up to our shoulders and the current so strong that one could barely stand. Thiwat seemed to have no difficulty in negotiating the swift flowing water, but Doereding and I were constantly on the brink of disaster. If either of us had slipped he would have been swept swiftly downstream. Since the river is filled with crocodile I could not help thinking that I was very likely to end up as luncheon delicacy. So much was I worrying about the crocodile that I positioned myself safely, or so I thought, downstream from Doereding and Thiwat on the theory that if crocodile swim with the current they should take them first and me later. This somewhat unheroic attitude was greatly appreciated by my companions, who, when they reached the bank, thanked me for my great courage in protecting them. As I appeared somewhat puzzled, Doereding explained that at this time of the year the crocodile generally swim upstream against the current, so unwittingly I had taken up the position of greatest danger. It seemed better not to disillusion my guides but on this occasion to pretend to have been a hero!

Having crossed the river we set out at a rapid pace through thick swamps with leeches constantly attaching themselves to our legs. Mosquitoes and flies bit; the heat intensified; my thirst became unbearable. Just when I was beginning to wonder if we should ever reach the fishing festival and when all three of us had lost every trace of festive feeling, we heard, in the distance, a low hum. Gradually the noise increased as we came upon a vast inland lake studded with black dots in motion. The warriors were coming our way, shouting and talking as they approached. We made a small mat of reeds to protect the camera and ourselves from the sun, and then squatted beneath it to rest from the exertions of the morning. Before us was an incredible sight: some six hundred totally naked warriors leaping about in the water shouting and yelping "Wa, Wa, Wa, Wa," as they drove their spears deep into the mud. The object was to make such a noise both in and out of the water so as to drive the mud fish from one end of the lake to the other. These fish wriggle or swim on the bottom of the lake and tend to hide in the mud when approached. Every once in a while a Nuer would raise his spear with a wriggling fish attached. These he would hand to a fish carrier wading along behind him. Two types of fishing spear were in use—a straight spear with an iron spike about 2 feet long attached to a wooden shaft, and a strange bow-like apparatus made up of a curved piece of wood held in shape by a piece of rope stretched taut, with a 2-foot iron spike attached to the end of it. The men with the straight spears drove them downwards as they walked through the water, but those with the bow-like weapons swung them from side to side. It was this second category which seemed to me the most dangerous for frequently they were known to succeed in spearing their neighbour's feet instead of the fish.

What an extraordinary scene lay before us: the sun shining on ebony bodies, the strange cries of the Nuer, some of them singing war songs, and the gradually increasing smell of the fish as they were dragged ashore. Some of these were about 20 pounds in weight and had huge whiskers. Thiwat claimed that mud fish are an aphrodisiac, highly regarded amongst his people. Having watched for some time it became so alluring that we all abandoned our goods—including my cameras—and joined in—Thiwat and Doereding borrowing from friends the more complicated type of fishing spears, whilst I contented myself with a plain one. The water was cool and refreshing, although the mud was somewhat unpleasant, tending to hold me glued to the bottom of the lake. Most of the time the water came up to my waist. The Nuer were delighted with the idea of a strange naked white creature joining in and everyone wished me good luck. Perhaps my thrust was too slow or perhaps I was just unlucky, but after half an hour I had to admit that this type of random fishing was not exactly my forte. All around me men were successfully spearing fish but I never hit one.

When we emerged from the lake hundreds of Nuer were standing or sitting around, joking or singing songs. The sun was beginning to set for it must have been about five o'clock. There were dark clouds in the sky indicating that the rains were coming. Boys would by now be driving the cattle towards their villages. Meanwhile fish were being cooked on hastily prepared fires. We squatted there in the marshes contentedly cooking and eating fish. A crowd collected around me, everyone wanting me to taste a bit of their fish. Every different type was produced for inspection and there was general delight when they discovered that I actually enjoyed eating their food. Moreover when they saw that I ate with one hand digging the bits of fish from the spine and balancing the flesh between thumb and forefinger before popping it into my mouth, they were delighted that the foreigner had already learned so much. The younger children were kept at a distance and only when their elders had had their fill were the scraps thrown in their direction. They would suck the bones of the fish and scrape off any bits of flesh attached to the discarded skins, heads or tails.

In the middle of this feast there was a loud clap of thunder overhead. Thiwat and Doereding looked up and whispered anxiously that it was time to be on the move. No Nuer likes to get caught in a storm, for they fear that they will be hit by lightning when crossing the open plains and marshes. In fact a number of Nuer are killed in this way. As there are few trees or tall objects in the area, man tends to stand out as a lightning conductor. Anyone killed by lightning is considered to have been removed by the gods and their spirit from henceforth joins Kuoth Nhial or the 'Spirits of the Above'; but this is little consolation for none of them really believe in an afterlife. Life on this earth they believe is good, provided you are Nuer.

As we headed towards the river I realized with dismay that there would be another crossing. This time however there were so many of us that the men made a chain across the river helping each other over and posting guards up and down stream to beat the water with their hands to frighten away approaching crocodile. The last Nuer to emerge from the river were in a certain amount of danger but otherwise the crossing had been beautifully organized. I felt infinitely safer when travelling with a large group than wandering about on my own.

With unexpected abruptness the rains broke: thunder and lightning were followed by a downpour as we rushed towards shelter. We had crossed the river at a point near the Anuak village where I had previously tried to borrow a canoe. Gar Quot who had now joined us, insisted that a few of the leaders of the Nuer, plus Doereding and myself, should demand shelter in this village. The Anuak chief, a wisened and unattractive old man, disliked the idea, but, realizing that he was surrounded by some six hundred Nuer, all potential enemies, considered it better to offer hospitality to the leaders rather than to be invaded by the rest. He was frightened by the presence of so many armed men surrounding his village.

He led us to his own hut where he offered us white beer. Unfortunately Anuak beer in my view is bitter and unpleasant compared with that prepared by the Nuer. After several Nuer had tried it by sucking through a straw they must have come to the same opinion, for one by one they ungraciously spat the beer on to the floor. I felt we should make some show of gratitude to our host, but was warned by Doereding not to be too polite to the Anuak. After all, he said, they are inferior people and it is their duty to provide us with what we demand, "For we are Nuer, brave men and the followers of Wiu."

Rain continued to fall but the thunder and lightning passed overhead. Gar Quot decided we should be on our way. We divided into groups of twenty to thirty, each party being protected by several men carrying rifles or spears. The fish were slung on sticks threaded through their gills and resting on the shoulders of pairs of the accompanying children. We walked fast as the light began to fade and the moon to glow dully behind the rain clouds. At moments we sang to keep up our spirits but at other times, when passing through areas considered to be hostile, we remained silent.

Normally I would have collapsed from exhaustion long ago, but I had felt that I could not let the Nuer see a white man overcome by weakness and had carried on in spite of the fact that I had drunk virtually nothing all day, apart from a few unrefreshing sips of Anuak beer. Perhaps my meal of Nuer fish had given me unexpected reserves of energy after all. But I think what really kept me going was the companionship of the Nuer, and the feeling of almost total acceptance which I had got from them during the long day together.

Kiir met us upon our return to Gwal Diok, helped carry in our fish and then cooked an evening meal. As I was about to eat he reminded us of the spirits and the need to attend to them first. So on either side of the hut offerings were left, for surely the spirits had helped us and deserved to be rewarded. The 'Man of Buk' or village elder had prophesied a good day's catch, and Buk, the spirit of the fish in the water, had answered his prayers.

God of the Sacred Spear

CHAPTER 7

Nyakwoth kot, Nyakwoth kot—
Go to Ciemgreng, where the people will shout at you
Like an animal, because you (the sister of Deng) . . .
Are an evil eye.

(Nuer song.)

Evans-Pritchard in his book, *Nuer Religion*, refers to the powers of the evil eye, but suggests that this is only a minor danger of Nuer existence. Yet during my stay at Gwal Diok, amongst the eastern Nuer, there was constant reference to people who were supposed to possess the evil eye. The Nuer, surrounded as they are by 'Spirits of the Above' and 'Spirits of the Earth' find it necessary to indulge in constant sacrifice to propitiate these spirits. In war the warriors are confident of their powers of conquest, but in constrast their everyday life is conducted in constant humility—evil must be punished, the spirits must be propitiated and the evil eye driven away. The tribesmen feel the presence of evil everywhere, believing that it causes illness and death. Luckily, there are other factors working in favour of continued existence. There are the good gods represented on earth by the prophets of Kiir, Deng and Wiu. Again Evans-Pritchard was not able to see the prophets at work when he visited the tribes in the early 1930s, for at that time a number of these true leaders of the people had been imprisoned by the British administration. Yet the prophets represent the only real religion of the Nuer. The gods themselves cannot be said to be entirely of Nuer origin, for both Deng and Kiir are known amongst the neighbouring Dinka. Wiu itself may be a Dinka spear (although no Nuer would admit it), but in all probability it represents a more truly Nuer concept.

The 'Spirits of Above' and the 'Spirits of the Earth' can be fairly easily distinguished from one another, but there are also a vast number of middle-of-the-road spirits which had to be propitiated to avoid trouble. Totems, fetishes and symbols surround Nuer bodies and homes in bewildering variety. Gar Quot had a shrine outside his house to protect the tall strong chieftain from lightning. Thiwat had a grandfather who had been born with a crocodile and had therefore assumed the crocodile as his totem spirit. In this context Thiwat really believed that his grandfather had been conceived together with a crocodile out of the same womb. Because of this extraordinary belief he and his family would never taste the flesh of crocodile or inflict any harm on these reptiles. When Evans-Pritchard discussed this very problem he went into great detail as to exactly what a totem spirit means to a family. For instance, does a Nuer really believe that a crocodile is a spirit or does he imply that some form of symbolism exists, rather like trans-substantiation. To my mind this type of analysis of Nuer thought is far too sophisticated. When I asked Thiwat if he thought the crocodile was a spirit he said, "No", but later, after having refused the flesh of crocodile he was equally able to explain that he could not eat it because it *was* a spirit. This is perhaps a typical example of Nuer self-contradiction. On the first occasion he probably did not want me to think that a crocodile was some form of god, but when it came to the point of being presented with the flesh to eat, superstition was the stronger force preventing him from doing something which he had been taught as a child was wrong. Similarly, Nyathiang had had her difficulties in life because of one single moment of weakness, when as a small girl, she had picked up a stone and carried it away—thus causing her to be barren for the rest of her life. One could go through the private histories of every individual in Gwal Diok. Without exception each family had a history of success or disaster dependent upon their relations with the good or evil spirits.

The spear represents survival and plays an important part from the time of manhood through to death—spear names being of almost equal importance with hereditary names in some areas. The second force, which is constantly present and also decidedly associated with each individual Nuer, is that of cattle. Not only do these pastoral people live and move with their cattle but a strange relationship builds up between man and beast. A boy will always have a favourite ox, to whom he sings, whose horns he twists into weird shapes and whose name he adopts after maturity. Every Nuer amongst the eastern clans appeared to have a cattle name by which he was known to his friends, though it was a matter of choice whether these names were used or not. Kiir, for instance, was a real name, but Doereding was a name taken after the colours of the ox which had been sacrificed at the time of his maturity.

Each of the three main gods has a definite function to perform in securing prosperity. Kiir, being the god of origin to whom all Nuer trace their families, is supposed to have arisen out of a green gourd floating down the river. The second major deity is Wiu, god of the sacred spear, and this cult was perhaps easiest for me to observe since Gwal Diok was so near the village of Wiu. Finally, Deng represented the god of fertility and rain, but probably has most to do with the planting of crops. Each of these gods is supposed to have one prophet at a time but schisms frequently occur; recently entirely separate Sudanese and Ethiopian cults have started to develop. The great spear itself tends to multiply so that there are lots of little Wius knocking around. It would seem that the gods vary in importance according to the condition of the tribes. When Evans-Pritchard lived amongst the Nuer, Deng was probably the most important force, but with the war in South Sudan Wiu has recently taken over from Deng, in much the same way as one might expect a god of war to oust a god of peace during a time of national crisis.

All three gods relate their activities to cattle and readily accept sacrifices. The character of the ruling prophets can often affect the popularity of the cult in a particular area. For instance, in Gwal Diok there was no doubt that Kor Jum, the prophet of Wiu, was regarded as a man of great power who was in contact with the 'Spirits Above'. On the other hand, the prophet of Deng who lived a short distance away was regarded as something of a joke. He drank, I suspect, a considerable quantity of alcohol, and had little authority apart from telling the people when they should sow the seeds of their crops. On one occasion the prophet of Deng appeared at my hut in Gwal Diok, together with his daughter who was suffering from a kidney disease. He was down-hearted and told me that if I could guarantee the cure of his daughter he would become a Christian and give up his religion. After explaining that I was not a missionary, that I would never ask him to give up his religion, and that anyway, alas, I could not cure his daughter, I watched him limp sadly away to return to his village.

Sacrifices to protect the cattle and people from disease occurred daily during my stay in Gwal Diok. Evidence of superstition was to be seen everywhere. Not only are crocodiles adopted as family totems but snakes, hippopotami, fish, lion, hyena, gazelle, elephant, giraffe and even inanimate objects such as trees, stones and grass. Nor are the prophets the only men with supernatural powers. There are leopard-skin priests who have special duties to exorcize the spirits of the dead—their function being to remove the gall bladder from an animal which has been sacrificed, as a propitiation for murder. These men, if they do their job properly, can prevent family feuds for they determine how many head of cattle should be paid to the relations of the deceased as a penalty for murder.

Next, there are a series of lucky charms such as shells or stones. Kor Jum was given to presenting iron bracelets for good luck. In my case he was to give me a splendid engraved metal band with a charm attached to prevent me from being murdered at night, so he said. There are also spirits contained in birds which should be avoided. No good Nuer ever eats a bird, although recently some tribesmen have secretly taken to eating the occasional chicken, explaining that as a chicken cannot fly it is not really a bird. Twins are referred to as having a special relationship, indeed as being a manifestation of the 'Spirits Above'. Lightning is something to be feared, hence the vast number of shrines to the spirits for protection. Dreams, curses and the evil eye are constantly frightening the people, and, above all, death terrifies the Nuer. To die as a warrior is one thing, but to die of sickness is thought to be a punishment from the spirits because the household did not pay enough attention to supernatural powers. Seldom is it possible to witness the burial of Nuer, for they are buried quietly by their own families at night beside their huts with the head nearest the door. People do not watch the burial, nor is it considered polite to refer to death, except when it occurs in battle.

Sometimes a whole neighbourhood can be affected (so they believe) by the improper conduct of a member of the community. Incest or adultery are crimes which can produce terrible retribution from the supernatural powers. Incest amongst the Nuer is so widely interpreted that all forms of cousin relationships are banned, together with nearly all other family relationships however distant. But if incest has a wider definition than in European communities, adultery has a narrower one—meaning literally the stealing of someone else's wife. A married man is totally free to have intercourse with as many women as he may wish, provided they are not the wives of his friends and associates. A considerate wife will, when pregnant, dash out to find a suitable unmarried female companion for her husband during the period of her pregnancy.

When disaster hits a particular area, the prophets, or more minor religious functionaries, the leopard-skin priests, are called in, the spirits are contacted and suggestions made as to how they can be propitiated. Sometimes families resist the advice of the prophets or priests, but inevitably further disasters then befall them. The longer they are postponed the more expensive the final sacrifices demanded by the spirits are likely to become. Should the initial sacrifice not achieve its objective there is always room for further sacrifices, until the family abandons all hope, reaching the conclusion that its sins are so great that the spirits will not be appeased. Although Nuer do not believe in an afterlife or a 'happy hunting ground', there is no doubt in their minds about the omnipresence of the spirits. Libations, hymn singing and sacrifices all take place in a recognized order. The sacrifices themselves fall into a sequence of four events: the presentation of the animal, its consecration, the invocation, and finally the immolation either by means of the spear or by suffocation. Meanwhile the spear, in the hand of the prophet or priest performing the function, is an extension of his right arm—his personality and power. Professor Westermann regarded these sacrifices as some form of "commercial bargain" with the spirits, but if one wished to draw a comparison it would seem fairer to view the sacrifices more in the nature of Christian prayer. No one expects them, even for their own good, to work all of the time, but everyone hopes that the 'Powers Above' will pay attention to the particular plea of that moment.

Inevitably Nuer religion leads to the subject of Nuer law, since religion itself is perhaps the basis of the social structure. Man, cattle and man's behaviour are all united in a self-administered society—self-administered by the Nuer according to a pre-conceived idea of correct behaviour. Let no one, therefore, say that primitive man lives a free and easy existence with no rules and regulations. The spirits are hard taskmasters. Exhausted as one may be after a day out fishing or a day in battle, the spirits nevertheless have to be looked after. When we returned from the fishing festival, it will be remembered that Kiir and I placed some of the best morsels of fish on the right and left side of my hut. These were for the spirits of Biel and Maluth. He had explained to me that first the spirits must eat, then we would be able to have our own meal. So it was that the village of Gwal Diok lived from day to day by constant attention to detail and careful reference to the divinities before any action was undertaken.

Kor Jum sacrifices a goat for the author

(*top*) The author's ox lies dead. (*bottom*) The ox meat is divided

A Stockbroker becomes Rial Nyang

CHAPTER 8

> Yeeah. . . . The world is mine, do not speak so loud
> my people. If I curse somebody, his rights will be
> stripped from him.
> When I return the brave are afraid; when I charge they
> scatter like women. Yet compare not my bravery with the
> power to which Deng Kur has testified—or the power of
> Wiu, which enables us to conquer Dinka and Anuak bringing
> them under our dominion.
>
> (Nuer War Song.)

A light breeze caused the grass to ripple across the open plain and swamps. The morning air was fresh and pure after yet another night spent lying on the ground on my goatskin bed. The rats had, as usual, kept me company, running over my legs and chest or nibbling at my cameras, before a bellow sent them scuttling back into the straw roof from where they would peer down at me throughout the night, twitching their whiskers when caught in the beam of my torch. There was consolation in the thought that where there are rats the snakes stay away, at least temporarily.

Outside a young boy stood beneath a urinating cow washing himself in the warm flow. Unsavoury perhaps, but after the chill of the night a warm shower was doubtless welcomed.

Doereding was still lying on his goatskin in the far corner. He looked much older than when we had set out ten days ago. His shorts and shirt were dirty and torn, his hair had grown grey with dust—and when he woke his eyes were red and bloodshot, the result, I suspected, of a hangover. As the sun began to rise a number of sick could be seen limping towards Gwal Diok. They had to be turned away, for had I begun to treat a single patient it would have been impossible to stop, and today had to be kept free for a very special ceremony. There was still a little Nescafe in the bottom of the only tin. An English breakfast might fortify me for the coming events, so I decided to make a brew of sugar and coffee together with hot milk from a nearby cow.

This was to be the day of my sacrifice to the pagan god of Wiu. An ox would have to be slaughtered and presented to the gods. Only in this way could I hope to become accepted by the prophet as one of his disciples. It would also help cement my increasingly close relationship with the inhabitants of Gwal Diok. More important, it might secure for me wider recognition amongst the Nuer—and enable me to help the sick in different areas. By making a sacrifice I would provide meat for the people at my own expense and prove to the prophet of Wiu that I had not just come to Gwal Diok to laugh at the customs of the people, but to join them. I was to be placed on trial and the gods would decide if I were in a fit state to be accepted. Should the decision be negative, I would probably have to leave the Nuer, at least in this area—but in the event of success I hoped for closer integration. These were the stakes and I had decided to take the gamble.

Certain preparations had been made beforehand. Thiwat and I had searched neighbouring villages for several days to find an ox suitable for an offering. Eventually he had selected a miserable beast owned by a friend, and it was not until Doereding had declared its unsuitability, that Thiwat produced a splendid animal with multi-coloured speckles for $150 Ethiopian (about £25 Sterling)—a high but still reasonable price for a really good animal. The night before it had been tethered near my hut and a fire of dung lit to keep off the flies and mosquitoes. Kiir, always instrumental in looking after my interests, tied a small reed tassel to its right horn for good luck. My fate and that of the ox were to be inexorably linked, through the coming events—the animal acting as a messenger between the spirits and myself.

Obtaining the permission of the prophet of Wiu, Kor Jum, to make a sacrifice had not been easy. Very seldom are outsiders allowed to undergo this ancient Nuer ceremony. The prophet had at first refused to meet me and all negotiations had taken place through Doereding and the prophet's brother. The reluctance of the Nuer to let me undergo this trial can probably be explained by their fear that I might fail. The danger would come should the gods decide that I were evil, and then the villagers would have to drive me out with sticks. Worse still the gods might decide that the smallpox epidemic, the lack of rain this year or some other disaster, was my fault. In which case they could demand that the death penalty should be swiftly executed. Such violence to a foreigner would be rare, but by applying to be allowed to sacrifice to the pagan gods, I had placed myself at their mercy. This was enough to make me decidedly apprehensive. I was in fact trembling in anticipation of the coming ordeal.

An hour went by. I suppose it must have been 6 am by now—my watch had long since ceased to function. I wondered if the men would really turn up, as arranged by Thiwat or whether they go about their daily routine as usual. Doereding then discovered the main singer heading off to fish and some of the others were slipping away. Soon there would be no one left in the village but women and children, and my sacrifice would be impossible. I tried to see Gar Quot, but was told he was sleeping. I went to the entrance of his hut demanding to see him. He appeared somewhat crest-fallen when I explained that he had promised that his men would accompany me to the sacrifice today—'Was Gwal Diok now to be disgraced before Wiu? Was the prophet Kor Jum to be kept waiting in vain? Was Gar Quot himself too feeble to command his people?" The last remark did it, with a roar Gar Quot rushed to the drums hanging in the centre of the village and started beating them himself. The men returned. It soon became clear why everyone had gone off. Since I had made no move, the village had assumed that I had decided to postpone the sacrifice to another day; or at least so they said.

Years ago a misguided missionary had attempted to end the cult of Wiu, and after being shown the sacred spear had stolen it under cover of darkness and hurled it into the river. The Nuer believe the spear rose again to return to its shrine—as is evidenced by its presence today. At any rate the missionary was, according to the Nuer, caught and killed by the tribesmen—who had from then onwards understandably kept foreigners at a distance. Since my arrival in Gwal Diok the prophet had proved elusive. For three days no one knew where Kor Jum was, or at least no one had been prepared to tell me. The men of Gwal Diok said that Kor Jum was a man of peace. When he walked between fighting tribes, planting his spear in their midst, the battle ceased. Kor Jum they claimed frequently became possessed of the spirit of Wiu and went into trances from which he spoke with the god's voice. Yet, I was warned Kor Jum was a strange man. He would demand presents of meat, goats or even cattle—or would remove ivory or iron bracelets from their owners. These he would not keep for himself (unlike many former prophets who had enriched themselves and their families), but, like a modern Robin Hood, he took from the rich to give to the poor. I was also told that Kor Jum must be humoured; if in a bad mood he would hide away in his hut refusing all visitors. At conferences, if the words were not pleasing to his ears, he would pretend to be deaf, forcing everyone in turn to shout out their case to him. The prophet of Wiu was obviously someone to be approached with care. The question uppermost in my mind was how would he take to me?

The men of Gwal Diok were now gathering around the hut, where my British flag flew triumphantly attached to the totem pole. Since we had to be covered in order to appear before Wiu, (for to appear naked before him is to invite sterility), I dressed in my best long trousers, a khaki shirt and a pair of sandals. A small gold crucifix, which frequently hangs around my neck, completed the attire. I felt that Wiu would not really mind this tribute to the

Christian God and I also believed that the Christian God would not mind terribly about my sacrifice to Wiu. Five or six villagers sat on skins outside waiting for others to assemble. Everyone had donned their best cloak or pair of shorts—the constant high-pitched chatter of native voices kept my thoughts far away from the price of ICI on the London Stock Exchange or the level of the Dow Jones Index.

The chief singer had just arrived, a hatchet-faced little man with a raucous voice. Soon we were nearly thirty in all, as Thiwat had succeeded in rounding up most of his relatives. Gar Quot wore a pair of blue trousers, an old shirt and carried his special aluminium stick. After a short choir practice, or warming-up session, we set off, Thiwat leading the ox with a grin a mile wide on his face. "*Wiu ee gorks, wiu ee gorks—la nei a nak jang,*" sang the warriors as they marched forward, some carrying their spears. The Nuer were asking Wiu to help them in fighting foreigners and to extend the tribe by the capture of Anuak and Dinka. They sang the prophecy of Wiu and the Gaajaak clan; that by colonization they would spread the power and glory of their god. The high-pitched scream, which precedes each verse and is uttered by the main singer, warned every village we passed that a sacrificial procession was on the way. The remainder of the men would then chant the response in an undertone before the next screech was uttered. It always puzzled me how any human being could consider this noise beautiful, yet my Nuer friends thought it the height of vocal achievement!

The sun was now rising and the clouds had blown away as we approached the village of the prophet. In the distance I could see a series of sticks cut into weird shapes which were planted in the ground in a large semi-circle. Various relics such as pieces of dried meat, leopard skins and drums hung from these. We stopped under a tree some hundred yards away sending an envoy to find the prophet. At first no one was able to find him. His brother bade us wait at a distance. More delays—one had to learn to be patient here.

I sat with Gar Quot and the other villagers of Gwal Diok. To pass the time we sang hymns but the words now changed from those of praise of a deity to descriptions of war. The two are so intertwined in Nuer philosophy that I suppose it is logical to sing of killing the enemy when approaching the sacred spear; but I could not get away from the feeling that we were not singing the right sort of song, rather like a school boy who starts putting crude words to "Onward Christian Soldiers!" The Nuer doubtless had no such misgivings. At one moment the words related to an account of an attack by buffalo, at another to the spearing of an enemy, "I spear Gawal and they become completely dead; I praise myself and say it is well done; I spear someone again and he dies at once; he is lost; he is lost; he is gone for ever." Then a verse told the "sons of slaves" to leave their homes and cried out for the children of Wiu to rule, "In my heart I want to do mischievous things, yet we have a real Prophet who is strong, that is why no one will be able to defeat us. If you run, Wiu will follow you and you will meet your fate during the night. We enjoy killing the enemy whom we will leave dead on the battlefield. . . ." Perhaps I was right to be worried about my fate!

Kor Jum's brother re-appeared. Permission had been granted to enter the village, so the procession got under way again. As we neared the hut in which the sacred spear was kept a considerable reception committee was waiting—all the male relations and subjects of the prophet were seated on the right of the hut. My villagers were placed on the left where they settled in a semicircle. I was taken to the centre of a large open space, which had been cleared of sticks and vegetation, facing both the temple of Wiu and equidistant between the relations of the Prophet and my own villagers. I felt very lonely as I sat cross-legged on the ground on a goatskin. Thiwat brought the ox and tethered it nearby. Then once again we settled down to a long period of waiting whilst the villagers continued hymn singing—now of a more reverend nature; the relations of the Prophet occasionally joined in. The main singer lept to his feet and pacing backwards and forwards let out his screeches as before. The voices of the warriors rose and fell in harmony. A grey-haired man cast some ashes over the ox. With a spear in his right hand he went through an invocation which is the first part of any Nuer sacrifice. I felt that I ought to be doing something myself, so rose to my feet and peered at the ox with sympathy. This also seemed an excellent moment to take a few photographs.

Then, when I was least expecting it, there was a roll of the drums and Kor Jum ran into the clearing. I was later to learn that his appearances were nearly always dramatic. At first I was disappointed by the prophet. He was wearing a leopard-skin and carried a handsome spear in his right hand whilst in his left he waved a fly whisk. But his face was riddled with smallpox scars and one eye was almost entirely closed. What a strange choice for a leader. As he weaved his way on to the scene, he lurched towards me. The whisper went round that Kor Jum was possessed of the spirit. At first he said nothing but charged towards me stopping with his spear about a foot from my chest. This strange sinister-looking priest of the pagan religion stared at me for some time with his one bleary eye, then hissed and spat in my face. This was not a mark of disapproval but quite a normal greeting from a great man, as I was told later. The next few minutes were equally filled with surprises as Kor Jum first rushed towards the villagers shouting at them to sing, then charged back towards me, hissing and making threatening gestures with his spear and fly whisk. Several times he stopped, peering at me so closely that his face was only a few inches away from my own. I could not help detecting what seemed to be a trace of the local alcohol on his breath. The drums had now ceased. Kor Jum approached his brother and bringing him to the circle demanded that a goat should be produced and sacrificed. A violent argument ensued with Kor Jum threatening to curse his brother if he failed to obey his command. The brother began by getting the better of the argument, then gradually gave way and disappeared reluctantly to bring back a fine-looking goat. Ashes were cast upon it before, taking his spear, Kor Jum cut its throat. This was a mark of esteem, Kiir whispered, since Kor Jum had said that if, as a foreigner, I could bring a fine ox to be sacrificed to Wiu, the least he could do would be to sacrifice a goat for me. Kiir had now joined me and quietly sitting by my side seemed prepared to share my fate. It was good to have a friend.

With the blood of the goat still dripping from his spear Kor Jum started prancing around the ox, upsetting the animal no end. At any moment it looked as if it might break away from the tethering peg which had only been lightly driven into the ground. Then, with a sudden thrust to the heart of the ox Kor Jum plunged his spear deep into its side and withdrew it. For a few seconds it looked as if he might have missed his target; nothing happened. Then blood began to pour from its mouth as gradually it sank to its knees, finally collapsing to the ground, its head pointing towards Wiu. The ox had decided my fate, for had it fallen to the west or with its head away from Wiu, I would never have been received into the tribe. True it had fallen on its left-hand side instead of its right, but this fact could be overlooked. So much is the animal connected with human beings in Nuer life that Evans-Pritchard wrote in *Nuer Religion* "When a Nuer gives a sacrifice he gives a part of himself". The behaviour of the animal as it died was meant to be a reflection of my own behaviour, whilst the colour of the ox was later to provide me with my Nuer name. As the poor animal lay dying on the ground, I realized what a strange ceremony I was witnessing. So far all had gone well.

It had now passed midday; the drums were beating again. I felt somewhat dizzy due to the sun and the smell of blood, but had I known what was about to take place I would have felt even less well! Several men rushed forward with knives and began to divide the meat. The procedure is clearly laid down by Nuer custom, for each individual has a right to a certain section of the meat. The basic principle is that one half should go to the villagers of Gwal Diok, the other, to the relations of the prophet. Having effected the initial distribution, individual pieces of meat would then be re-distributed—the old men receiving the tender parts whilst the young would be given more muscular cuts.

After all the meat had been cut, the head of the ox was laid in front of the hut of Wiu. An argument began over distribution. Initially the pile belonging to Gwal Diok appeared to be bigger than that of the prophet, but some troublemakers continuously transferred pieces from one pile to the other, accompanied by violent abuse and physical restraint. Kor Jum, who up until now had kept apart from the rather undignified scene, then removed all the meat. There was a howl of rage from the men of Gwal Diok as they saw their dinners disappear. Kor Jum stood smiling with spear in hand, a fine example of the power of Wiu incarnate. Having had his little joke, he then allowed the division to continue. I sent Doereding into the fray to try to ensure a fair distribution, for normally it would have been up to me as the person making the sacrifice to ensure everyone's rights. I felt totally inadequate to deal with this situation; Doereding on the other hand was only too keen to become involved in anything which might gain him the favour of our village. Kor Jum took me gently by the hand, leading me towards the hut of Wiu, perhaps, I thought, to get me out of the way. His brother and one other man moved aside the straw door concealing the entrance to the temple and I crawled in behind the prophet.

At first my eyes were not accustomed to the dark and I could see nothing. There was only the unpleasant smell of decayed meat and cattle grease. Then in the centre of the hut I saw the huge spear of Wiu resting on a small wooden stool, blade downwards. Tied to the shaft were pieces of leopard skin and other strange symbols. The blade was covered with grease and at the foot of the wooden stool lay various offerings such as iron bracelets and some Ethiopian dollars. The prophet removed my shirt and I noticed he had brought into the hut some of the intestines of my ox as well as some of the fat. He smeared the intestines over me, then taking small pieces of raw fat rubbed them against the sword of Wiu. Opening my mouth he placed them on my tongue, instructing me to swallow. Four times I had to munch these loathsome bits of fat whilst wondering how long it would be before I should be violently sick. Next he took a small bowl of rancid butter and anointed my forehead, chest and arms. All this time I was alone in the hut with Kor Jum; two other Nuer were standing guard outside. He looked at me kindly and seemed to be giving me a blessing, muttering various incantations as he went through these rites. Finally he signalled me to leave the hut while he remained inside. Outside in the fresh air I tried to make my way to a lonely spot, where, without being seen, I could remove any bits of fat which still remained in my mouth. Alas, the Nuer were far too curious and surrounded me allowing no escape.

The division of the meat had been concluded amicably. It only remained to wait for Kor Jum to give the final dispersal instructions and his blessing. The prophet came out of the hut and grabbed one trembling warrior from my village, telling him that he had been disrespectful towards Wiu in the past year. The man certainly appeared terrified as Kor Jum forced him to come forward into the hut and prostrate himself before the sword. I could not see what happened inside but when he reappeared the villager was very subdued. Perhaps he had been given an '*hors d'oeuvre*' of the same variety as I had just experienced. That would be enough to quieten any warrior!

The drums beat again at the command of Kor Jum. Having closed the temple, he now stood before us all holding his own spear. There was complete silence from the crowd as he shouted the words "Rial Nyang." At first I thought this was some form of invocation until I realized that everyone was looking at me laughing and shouting, "Rial Nyang." This was to be my Nuer name. It referred to the colour of the ox which had just been sacrificed. The two words taken separately can mean a variety of things. But *Rial* here implied something multi-coloured. *Nyang* can be associated with a crocodile. Although I realized that the words taken together belonged to the ox, I could not get away from the idea that they were calling me a multi-coloured crocodile.

This seemed particularly appropriate when a few weeks later I did in fact shoot a 15-foot crocodile. I tried to explain this to the Nuer, but nobody knew what on earth I was talking about. To them Rial Nyang was either me or my ox.

There remained but one other privilege to come my way. As I started off towards Gwal Diok with the villagers carrying our share of the meat, I passed between two lines of men, who with great ceremony spat on my head. Afterwards I was assured that this was a great favour, indicating complete acceptance into the tribe. At that moment I could only feel thoroughly sick from the raw flesh that I had had to swallow. I could not get away from the idea that I must look rather ridiculous, still covered with bits and pieces of the ox's intestines and dripping with human spittle. So, making proper excuses, I allowed the villagers to go their own way and myself headed off to the river to try and wash away the smell of the sacrifice. Luckily I still had a small piece of carbolic soap in my pocket.

By rights Doereding and I should have made sure that our villagers got safely back with their meat. When we did return to Gwal Diok, we discovered that some of the meat had disappeared *en route*. Two or three tribesmen claiming part of the sacrifice had removed the pieces of rib and foreleg destined for me personally. To lose my dinner in this way was unfair and Doereding was beside himself with grief. So we set out with a party of four or five men to try and catch the thieves. As we came upon them in a neighbouring village, there was a shout of "Rial Nyang", and feeling that I had acquired some status in this society, I simply picked up the bits of meat lying unprotected on the ground in front of the hut, handed them to my men and went off with a foreleg of beef on my shoulder. There was no resistance and we returned happily to Gwal Diok singing on the way. That evening a proper feast took place and I was invited to visit almost every family hearth in the village. The girls came forward, peered at me, shouted "Rial Nyang," and ran away again. Even the children could not resist the temptation to crowd around shouting, "Rial

Nyang," shrieking with laughter as they discovered that I knew my name and might make some response. After a while I found that the easiest answer to "Rial Nyang" was simply the English word "Yes." This the children thought wildly funny. I am sure that even today there will be children in the village of Gwal Diok shouting the word "Yes" at their parents, in memory of Rial Nyang.

As the day ended I sat in front of Thiwat's mother's hut. They told me that had I been sick after the sacrifice or had the ox fallen facing the wrong way, I would never have received my name. Inevitably the conversation turned to Kor Jum and his relations. I asked who the next prophet would be if Kor Jum were to die (a subject not normally contemplated). How would he be chosen? According to Nuer Law, any senior member of the prophet's family could be selected to succeed him by the Wiu village. The office was hereditary but not under a system of primogeniture. It would go to the most able male member of the family, especially if he claimed to be possessed. In Kor Jum's case this would be his brother. It was the duty of the entire village to elect a prophet who would protect the sacred spear. There would always be men on guard to ensure that no one approached the area without permission. Should the prophet be away travelling amongst the tribes, the true spear still remains within the hut, protected by the inhabitants of Wiu village. Often travellers in other areas are shown other spears and told that they are the sacred spear—but in most cases the Nuer are simply pointing out the local representation of the real Wiu, which they know is elsewhere.

The night air was cool now and the fires were nearly out. Cow dung burned to keep the mosquitoes away from the beasts which coughed occasionally, assuring us of their presence. Just as I was preparing to turn in, Kor Jum came rushing into the village attended by four or five warriors. He was in high spirits in every sense of the word and came straight to where I was seated. The people moved aside to make room for him. He put his arm around my shoulder. From under a red cloth robe he drew a small iron bracelet with strange pieces of metal attached to it. This he placed around my wrist. The gift was meant to keep me from being set upon by enemies and murdered at night. The butter, which he had poured on me during the day, was meant to ensure my fertility. So now I was properly protected from the evil spirits. "You will have many children," he had assured me, and he seemed totally unabashed when I replied that I did not even have a wife. "That could easily be put right," he explained, "for anyone who could afford to sacrifice such a fine beast to Wiu had not only proved that he respected their god but also that he was a man of wealth who could afford to buy many wives." After a drink of aragy, Kor Jum left.

It was time to sleep. The dogs protecting the village barked aggressively, and then silence—save the tubercular coughing of an old man. Night had fallen on Gwal Diok and Rial Nyang.

A True Citizen

CHAPTER 9

The World is full of troubles and
The sons of slaves will leave their homes
Our village of Wiu will be ruled by us
For Wiu will protect us with his strength.
(Nuer—In Praise of Wiu.)

It is somewhat surprising to find the word 'slave' used in songs unless it is taken to be in direct contrast to the word 'citizen'. The children of 'Jang' refer directly to the descendants of people once captured by Nuer and colonized by them. Sometimes, after a successful battle an individual was captured, brought back and adopted into a family. Frequently, whole villages were brought under Nuer dominion. But the 'Jang' or sons of slaves do not walk around with chains or handcuffs. Today they are fully integrated into the society although first they may have to prove their worth. A Dinka living amongst the Nuer in the past may have imported some of his own customs and these have often appealed to his captors who have adopted them. In this way, no doubt, Deng first became a Nuer god-concept. Strangely enough, the captives are seldom recorded as having escaped or returned home—perhaps because their capture would in itself have been a disgrace amongst their own people, more probably because life with the Nuer was not an unpleasant experience. If captured young enough, they soon grew to accept their adopted parents. Sometimes captured men received garring as administered by the

Nuer (see Chapter 10) and at a later age, married and set up their own families. Only when it came to battles or decisions affecting the safety of the community were these adopted sons not entirely trusted. In their songs therefore 'sons of slaves' are depicted as slightly second-class citizens.

Stories such as that of Latjor perhaps best illustrate the colonizing spirit of the Nuer. Originally the tribes came from the west and most of the eastern clans are therefore descended from western groups. Latjor came from the west but promised the people that he would conquer the lands to the east. So under the banner of the 'spear' Latjor together with his warriors set out on their 'imperialistic' designs. Nuer folklore endows Latjor with all the qualities of a hero; courageous and intelligent employing just leadership. Before him and his men, the Dinka fled or were captured. The Shilluk (being a smaller tribe) were encountered, but since they were well organized under their king and had no cattle, Latjor did not bother to engage them in battle. The same would have been true of the Anuak, but unfortunately they stood in the way of Nuer progress. So alongside the Dinka they fought many battles with the bands of Nuer advancing from the west. When fighting the Anuak Latjor would employ tactics still used by the Nuer today in their battles against Sudanese army strongholds. He and his men would wait for the hottest time of the day, then at noon when the Anuak lay resting in their villages, the warriors would attack; for the Nuer believe they are better able to withstand the intense heat of the sun than other tribes. On other occasions the attacks would be aimed at achieving the maximum element of surprise, and they would take place in the early hours of the morning. In this way the Nuer conquered and spread eastwards, driving the Anuak and other tribes before them.

There is no disgrace attached to killing provided it is not one's neighbour and provided deaths are followed by the proper propitiation of the gods with sacrifices conducted by leopard-skin priests. Sometimes the battles that take place are merely retaliatory, sometimes they are caused by accidents such as the quarrelling of individuals, but more often they occur during raids conducted to capture cattle. Young men eager to purchase wives have first to find the bridal price. Wars take place to recapture girls stolen from a village or to revenge their seduction——shades of Helen of Troy. An Anuak youth was recently carried into hospital more dead than alive. He had fallen in love with a Nuer girl who appeared to return his affections. However, her ever-vigilant brother, mindful of his sister's honour, set a trap and caught the lovers together. With some friends they set about the Anuak with knives and spears, inflicting hundreds of cuts all over his body and leaving him to bleed to death in a ditch. He was found by native traders passing by and flown out of the area by plane to a hospital where his life was saved.

On another occasion, I was myself present when some Nuer elders came all the way to Gambela. They had entrusted their daughters to the local school—the first Nuer girls ever to come there—and they informed the young Peace Corps teacher called Candy that the girls had received improper letters. The elders could not read, but a few of these epistles had been found when the children returned to their village, where a student had read them aloud to a circle of listening tribesmen. The letters were unsigned but purported to come from a lover of one of the girls, who described in detail the joy of her seduction in the school's classroom after work. The elders had been enraged but allowed their daughters to return to school on condition that the offender was caught and punished. Back at the school the case of the 'pornographic letters' had been dropped after investigation, for it was thought that the boy who had composed the letters had been exercising more of his imagination than his sexual prowess. The elders heard of this unsatisfactory result and determined to seek retribution. They came to Gambela to kill the boy! No amount of persuasion would change their minds, and for several days they hung around the town waiting to pounce on the student in question, until the Ethiopian police eventually hustled

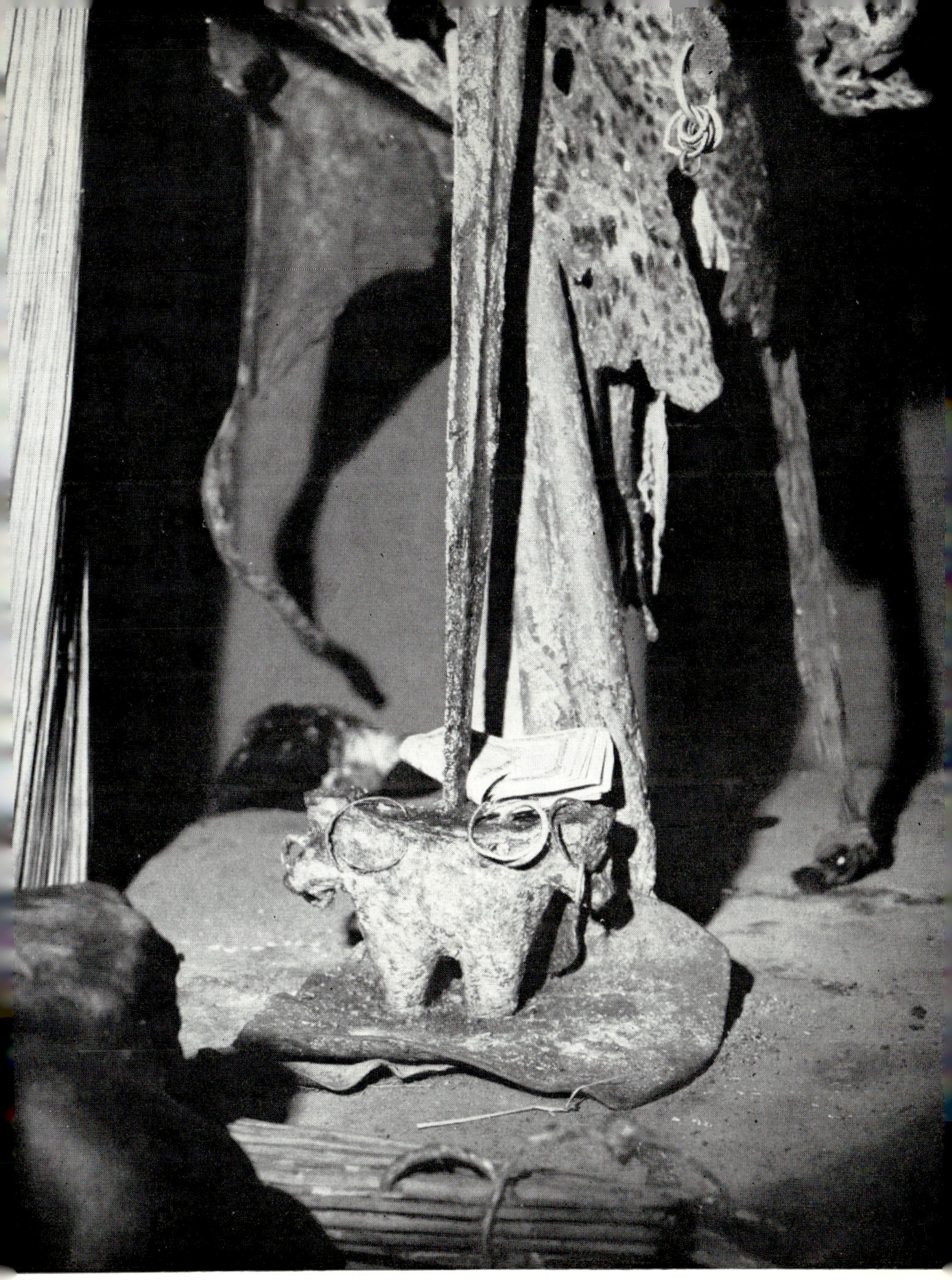

The sacred spear, Wiu

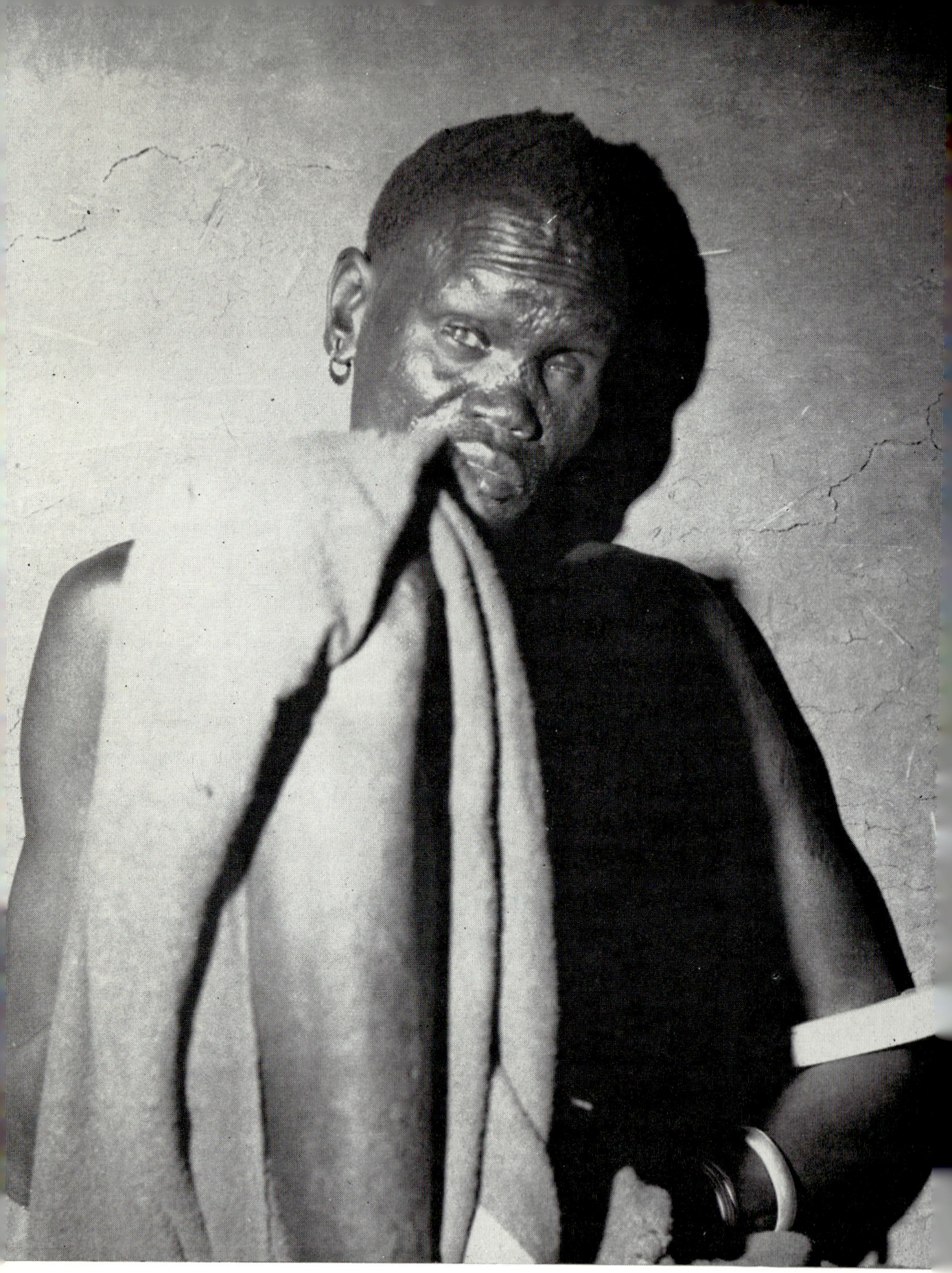

Kor Jum, the prophet of Wiu

them away threatening arrest. With them went the girls, sacrificing education for honour in Nuer eyes.

These anecdotes serve to illustrate the sense of honour prevailing. Women must be protected. Insults must be revenged lest the recipient be thought a coward. Bravery is an ingrained principle from the time of maturity to the hour of death. The Nuer are constantly ready for war—their type of war.

Whilst in Gwal Diok, Nuer warriors armed with spears and old-fashioned rifles constantly came and went on mysterious missions—mostly at night. They were often on their way to help the rebels (or Anya-Nya) in the Sudan. Prior to my arrival, there had been a particularly fierce battle on the plain involving a number of villages. The cause was never established, but I was given to understand that Gwal Diok had not been defeated. Twenty of the enemy who were also Nuer lay dead on the grass in the early hours of the morning; the rest of the attackers had fled. The prophet of Wiu had played an important role in putting an end to the fighting, for he had hurled his spear into the middle of the battle field declaring he would curse anyone who fired another shot or threw another spear. "It is not for the clans of Gaajock and Gajaak to fight each other. Save your strength for the common enemy." By this he indicated that the warriors should be fighting the North Sudanese troops, not each other.

Squabbles between clans have increased of late because of the overcrowding which occurs when thousands of refugees descend on those already grazing their cattle in an area. The complete breakdown of law and order in South Sudan, in so far as it previously existed under British district commissioners and officers, has encouraged bands of robbers to plunder without fear of capture. Added to this the Anya-Nya has sometimes been forced to demand food and supplies from the villages they visit in order to survive themselves. It can therefore be readily appreciated that the Nilotic peoples living under these conditions are reluctant to undertake journeys except when accompanied by a number of armed men.

The Ethiopian Amhara police, who are now responsible for patrolling the frontier area on the Ethiopian side, preferred to remain in the comparative safety of their compounds, making only occasional sorties into the countryside as a show of force. The same atmosphere prevailed on the Sudanese side of the border. There, the army felt safer barricaded inside the garrison towns where they could control the local inhabitants.

In this area which had seldom known prolonged peace, conquest was frequent, making a true citizen hard to define. He must be of pure Nuer blood, descended from the god Kiir. He must be free from any form of consanguinity, and this applies particularly to the abhorred sin of incest. So far-reaching is this concept of incest, as has been already explained, that it often requires the advice of a prophet to determine permissable relationships. The daughters of men in your own age group are taboo, for are you not brothers if you received garring together? (see Chapter 10)—and you cannot marry your brother's daughter! Cousins of all sorts are out and so naturally are parents, uncles and aunts, nieces and nephews, brothers and sisters etc. Remember that with fairly wide interpretation of the above, the number of people in the 'avoidance' categories is even greater. A man who is adopted into a family becomes an automatic relative. Moreover, such is the sin of incest that it debars one from citizenship forever.

Villages, like clans and tribes are built up by marriage and conquest, whilst the reputation and wealth of each village depends on the achievement of the individuals therein. War must be fair but successful, for a village which had suffered much illness or successive defeats will never be honoured. Nuer always know what is right according to their law and are amazed at the confusion of others! As has been written, Nuer law is self-administered according to preconceived ideas of correct behaviour. Each crime has to be judged by the community as a whole and sentence pronounced. Take adultery—the degree of sin committed would depend on how close a neighbour the offender turned out to be, but more particularly if he were caught in the act. An adulterer in one's own village might be killed if he were a constant offender, whilst someone from a distant town could escape with a beating by the husband and his friends, along with a fine of five or six head of cattle. It would largely depend on the quality of the insult. In some cases a Nuer adulterer of good family would be more easily forgiven than a foreigner, whose act might be interpreted as a direct attack on tribal pride. For instance Ethiopian Amhara police caught in the act would stand little chance of surviving the experience. If a woman is accused of adultery, she is expected to name her lover. Should she attempt to shield him, she can anticipate either continuous beating or being tied up with rope made out of rhino hide. The tying with leather rope is particularly painful, for when wet it expands, but when dried in the sun, it cuts into the flesh becoming tighter and tighter. The poor female will be roped all over and stretched out in the sun. Frequent buckets of water will then be thrown over her to relieve the pain of her bonds with the certain knowledge that each time they dry out the pain will be worse. I was told of a woman suspected of adultery who was roped to the ground and her fingers were broken one by one because she would not name her lover, but this I take to be an unusual occurrence. Public torture is not part of Nuer tradition, and most offenders get off with a good beating together with a fine.

Deviations on the other hand merit strong treatment. It surprised me to find that in an almost totally naked society, homosexuality was never discussed. "It is a bad thing, like death. We do not talk about it," they said. The penalty for a homosexual could indeed be death, for the act is thought of as a degrading Arab insult. Lesbianism puzzled them even more. "What do women do?" they asked, as I tried to explain my question. The only comment was, "How silly, and what a waste of time. We use our women when we want them; they need never lack a man". Male circumcision is also out. It is thought of again as an Arab custom. "There is no need", they told me "to create udders like a cow."

Inevitably, Nuer law is intermingled with Nuer religion, as has been seen in the penalties for murder and the use of leopard skin priests. Difficult cases are brought before the Prophets for judgement, particularly if they involve the divergent views of different communities. In these cases, the job of the prophet is to prevent the matter turning into a feud between two villages by providing a just solution. One must remember the Nuer are hypersensitive on the question of maintaining their honour. Thiwat had nearly stopped working for me when some of the local lads 'got at him' for consorting with a foreigner. Only Gar Quot's direct intervention by putting Thiwat 'on his honour' to protect me had saved the day. "You must be strong", Gar Quot had told Thiwat, "and not pay attention to the chatter of children. What the foreigner is doing is good for our people and it is your privilege to help him." Put that way, the whole matter took on a new aspect. Nothing must be taken for granted. The affections of a girl may be available, but this is a positive danger unless the family agrees and honour is maintained.

Theft is unusual amongst the Nuer, at least their interpretation of theft. Missionaries have often told me that the Nuer are the greatest thieves and brigands alive. But they fail to understand tribal customs when they make these accusations.

When I was living in Gwal Diok none of my possessions were ever touched, although my few clothes, cameras and the bottle of whiskey must have represented a considerable fortune to the villagers. On the contrary, if forgetfully I left my hut door open, Nyathiang or someone else would come to pull the reed matting across the opening to ensure the safety of my possessions in the event of outsiders entering the village. The only exception was the ram that Gar Quot's brother brought me which had been frequently removed, but then this had been an unwilling gift and the poor man was merely repossessing what had been his. However, when later on a European-type camp was established beside the Baro River, my guest status disappeared, as did a number of our belongings.

There is a strange (at least to us) Nuer dictum, and that is 'what is left around carelessly is available for all'. Take an incident which happened to Thiwat in my company. When bathing in the river, he left his straw hat on the bank. He forgot about the hat after his swim, and when he returned later to collect it, it was gone. Two days afterwards, we came across a small boy with Thiwat's hat pulled down over his ears. The child, his parents and relations all swore that it was their hat; for had it not been found thrown away on the river bank? By Nuer law they were right, and Thiwat was lucky to regain his property after several hours of argument. Fortunately for him, his hat was so well known in the district that countless witnesses could be produced to support his case—also, and more important, he was Gar Quot's adopted son. However, actual theft inside one's own village is not permitted and a culprit caught in the act can expect at least a good beating.

Children are severely disciplined by their elders. Before garring a boy can be ordered around by all the men in the village and instructed to undertake any chore. If he refuses, he can be beaten without reference to his parents. The only form of resistance I noted was when some children go on hunger strike in an attempt to get revenge on their parents. Two such children were dragged before me one evening in Gwal Diok: their parents had threatened that the white man would eat them unless they behaved. There was terror in their eyes as they were pulled, screaming and kicking, towards the white ogre, and the dinner was placed before them. I have never seen two dinners 'wolfed' so quickly, although afterwards I discouraged parents from the repetition of this performance, lest large numbers of children should grow up frightened of me, and believing in white cannibals. Children may be strictly controlled in some ways but they have a freedom in their games which might shock the modern world. One day I saw a boy and girl aged about 7 or 8 playing at marriage in front of their elders. They disappeared to the grass where they attempted to make love; seeing my surprise, the elders asked, "What harm can they do? No babies will result!"

Perhaps some indication of the standards required in daily life can be gained by describing the functions of a number of leading citizens in any one village. Apart from prophets, priests and (government-appointed) chiefs, there are a number of traditional roles to be played by men skilled in particular fields. The most important individual is usually the 'elder' of the village. He must be a 'true citizen' and someone to whom all can turn for advice and impartial judgement. In general he will be the senior member of the most important family in the area, and is liable to be rich in cattle—though there are exceptions to this rule. He may summon other elders together to discuss issues of importance, or he may decide to call on the prophets or priest for matters of a specifically religious nature.

Then there is the 'Man of Cattle' whose job is to protect the herds, giving advice as to their welfare and grazing. He may frequently be someone of great wisdom and his functions inevitably take on a religious significance. Remember, as the Nuer say laughingly, "We and the cattle see the moon first as it rises in the evening, long before the rest of humanity."

The 'Man of the Earth' has almost equally important functions though his status would normally be below that of the 'Man of Cattle'. Besides being the representative of the prophet of Deng in the village, the 'Man of the Earth' would for instance be present when confessions of adultery are sought. Should the offender, having been named, deny his crime, fearing punishment, the 'Man of the Earth' would then send for an animal to be sacrificed. Then in front of a large audience he would warn of the many dangers of deceiving the spirits. "Let the spirits punish the adulterer by casting the evil eye upon him. Let him sicken, his family fall into poverty, his cattle die, his heirs be cursed etc. . . ." The 'Man of the Earth' would drone on, his incantations becoming more and more horrifying, until either the adulterer or his friends would come forward begging that the curse should not be effected. Seldom is the animal sacrificed, for should its blood reach the earth without a confession being obtained, the adulterer would be doomed.

The 'Man of Garring' is another specialist, a surgeon who will be discussed at length in the next chapter. There is also the 'Man of Teeth', whose function is less that of a dentist and more that of an extractor. His job is to remove the two lower middle teeth from both boys and girls. This custom is common amongst the peoples of the Nile as well as amongst many of the pastoral tribes further South in Kenya and Uganda.

Numerous men and sometimes women are believed to have special associations with a particular spirit. Take the 'Man of Buk'. He would be expected to tell the villagers where and when to fish. Other individuals might be thought to be close to Biel or Maluth—these would normally be from families who had adopted these gods as their totems.

Finally there are the tradesmen such as the blacksmiths who make the knives and spears, the ropemakers, the thatchers, the hunters, the fishermen, the warriors, the herdsmen etc.

But all these trades, with the exception of that of the blacksmith, are practiced to a greater or lesser extent by most adult males in the village. Communal life leads to communal activity, although when any particular problem arises advice is frequently sought from the acknowledged expert.

Garring

CHAPTER 10

Our cows, our cows
They are part of ourselves
We take them to graze in fine pastures
We clean where they rest.
But we are leaving them now
When we become men.
Good to be a man, yeah
Good to be a man.
(Song of Garring.)

As a tribe the Nuer are distinguished by the marks which they received at their coming of age ceremony called garring. Although in the olden days this was a maturity ceremony, today boys of the eastern Nuer clans of Gaajock and Gajaak are normally given garring between the ages of 7 and 8. When Evans-Pritchard was studying the Nuer in the early 1930s, he found that the average age at which garring took place was between 10 and 12. The reason for the change is not altogether clear. Perhaps boys become men somewhat earlier nowadays, or perhaps their fathers fear that the custom may die out and wish to ensure that their sons participate before it is too late. To the Nuer garring confers a status marking the end of boyhood. Other tribes such as the Dinka have marks on their foreheads and bodies. Some clans of the Dinka even practice garring, but it does not have the same significance and is not done in the same way. (Dinka garring is sometimes carried out on both boys and girls, who for instance often remain in a sitting position.)

What happens at the garring ceremony is that the Nuer male child has six parallel lines cut into his forehead with a small knife. These marks remain with him throughout his life as a visible proof of maturity. The method which is used, the preparation beforehand, the period of isolation afterwards and the subsequent re-entry into male society, I was soon to witness in a small village several miles from Gwal Diok.

For the last ten days Gar Quot had been assuring me that his son would receive garring, but now he found a new series of excuses for avoiding the issue. The main problem was that somewhere in the Sudan he had corn that he wished to transport to the village. Until he was able to do this Gar Quot had very little interest in the subject of garring. How could he risk running out of food for his son? If, however, I were willing to go with him to fetch the corn (which would only take a couple of weeks) we would have a splendid garring party afterwards. Thiwat warned me that Gar Quot's corn was very far way, that we might spend a month not weeks searching for it, as well as endangering our lives, since it was thought to be stored in a village which had recently been raided by the North Sudanese army.

As with all things in Africa, luck is an important factor. My meeting with Muony was a complete accident—nor is there any reason why I should have discovered that Muony was a gaar, or man who gives garring. Thiwat, Kiir, myself and Doereding were all plunging about in a shallow pool beside the river Baro, cooling ourselves after the noonday heat. It was mid-afternoon and there was not a cloud in the sky.

Half a dozen small boys were busily engaged in jumping into the river. They plunged in, often landing on top of us, leaping from the bank above and landing with a great splash in the water below. There was no sophistication about attempting a dive—it was just a short run, a leap, and a splash which could be caused by anything from a belly-flop to arriving in the water in a statuesque position, hands raised above the head.

I was trying to introduce the Nuer girls to soap. At first these careful maidens had mistaken my innocent intentions in approaching them in the water. Kor Jum's wife, who was bathing at the time, told them that I meant no harm—and gradually curiosity brought them nearer. They watched me with growing fascination, firstly because I was so hairy, and secondly because of the foam that collected as I rubbed myself with the bar of soap. One or two of the bolder girls came up to us—laughing, but always moving away when I tried to grab them. Doereding was swifter off the mark, and catching one golden brown beauty with firm breasts, he forcibly gave her a soap bath all over. The noise was fantastic; she struggled and screamed and squirmed—but when released, returned to her girl friends to be admired. They must have been impressed by the smell of the soap—for from that moment onwards we had plenty of candidates for soaping! Nor was it all one-sided. In return for the use of our soap, they were only too willing to suggest the service of washing us. This they did, and very thoroughly, with no embarrassment. Such it is to live in a society free from inhibitions—not a totally permissive society, but one which does not prohibit or disapprove of men and women bathing nude together in a river.

These girls were enjoying the freedom nature intended. All they wore in the water were beads around their necks and waists and ivory cut into arm and leg bands. On the river bank, they had stacked their pots for carrying water or grain—to be collected after their swim. It was a happy occasion, so long as the crocodiles kept away!

Muony passed by and seeing us in the water, smiled and shouted a few words of greeting. He had come a long way, for his greying hair was covered in dust. We left the cool of the river and rested in the shade of a tree. Muony told us that 'the knife was out', meaning that tomorrow morning he would be giving garring to several boys in a neighbouring village. This elderly Nuer—he might have been somewhere between 50 or 60—had a kind smile. He was the sort of man one would trust automatically. Had he been a doctor in Europe, Muony would have been accredited with a bedside manner. As it was, in Africa, the children liked him because he never had a cross word to say to anyone. I was later to learn that it is extremely important to choose a 'Man of Garring' who is skilled, for not only does he leave his mark on tribesmen for the rest of their lives, but their very survival depends on the steadiness of his hands as well as his ability to sever the nerves correctly, cutting the veins in the right place. Nor must he be squeamish, for the knife must penetrate deep into the very bone of the skull otherwise the cuts will turn septic.

That evening we set out to reach the village where the initiation would take place.

After the usual gift of white beer, we talked to the parents of the boys about to 'come of age'. Knowing something of the horror of the ceremony I was surprised at the eagerness with which the boys rushed to meet Muony, explaining how they longed to have their heads cut. A number of children who could not have been more than 5 or 6 years old came forward begging to be allowed to become men, only to be rudely pushed aside by their relations. Nuer children do not often cry, but these small boys allowed the tears to pour down their cheeks. By this time the entire village had gathered around us whilst Muony explained how busy he had been during the last few weeks moving from place to place performing his art.

There was a communal spirit about the whole affair. When one realizes that ultimately it must be the choice of the children themselves, one can see that this is a typical example of a community setting a standard which an individual automatically accepts. For example, the parents of the boys concerned would not have ordered their children to be garred, but probably for the last year or so they would have been making remarks such as, "I wish this boy would become a man." Equally, their girl friends would have said to them, "After you are garred we will be able to go with you to dances but now you are still a boy." It is hard to tell which would be the greater incentive, the suggestive remarks of the parents or the jibes of girl friends.

Preparations for the garring were well underway. Beer had been brewed and a considerable amount of food had been stored by the families concerned.

The boys themselves are often responsible for negotiating their fee with the gaar. It crossed my mind that if any child were a bit mean about his offerings, the consequences might be unfortunate. Muony did not ask much for his services—food, a spear and a cloak—that was all.

I caught sight of one small boy whom I had tried to treat for yaws a few days before. He had then, in a mystifying manner, refused to allow me to give him an injection of penicillin. I had been irritated at the time, not understanding why, if he had bothered to come all the way to see me with this unpleasant disease, he steadfastly refused to be treated. Now I understood. He was to receive garring tomorrow; had he had an injection from Rial Nyang he would have been accused of being given drugs to lessen the pain of the head-cutting. Nor was I able, during his period of isolation, to give him any further medical attention, other than to blow a little disinfectant powder on the wound.

As we sat in the evening twilight talking to Muony, the boys began singing spontaneously. They were chanting some of their childhood songs for the last time. I could not catch many of the words. But one song was a particular favourite of this village. The small girls sat in another group clapping their hands together or against their bodies in unison. Each child in turn sang a verse ending always with the chorus which we all chanted, "*Oh-hey da da ding-jar-dey, oh-hey da da ding-jar-dey.*" I cannot translate any of the words, which my Nuer friends tell me are meaningless, but I retain not only the memory of the children singing in their squeaking voices with all the uncertainty of immaturity, but also an excellent tape recording of the song in question.

The boy with yaws sat next to me, gazing at the stranger, probably wondering if I was going to bring him good or bad luck. The parents chatted, coughed and spat as they sat around the camp fire. Meanwhile I asked to be allowed to film the head-cutting in the morning. Without realizing what I asked, I suggested that the ceremony should take place as late as possible in the day so that there would be sufficient light for my cameras. It was only when the whole ghastly process was over, that I learnt from Muony, it is extremely dangerous to cut heads once the sun has fully risen. For this means that the heart beats faster, causing the children to lose more blood. Garring should always be done in the cool of the morning before the sun rises or in the evening, so long as there is no wind around to blow dust into the wounds and cause infection. Nor did I know at this time the consequences of having the wounds go septic, for the only solution to this is to cut them open again so that the infection is bled away. Sitting around the fire, and chatting about how the boys would soon become men, no one thought of these unpleasant things. In the morning, the reputation of the various families would be at stake, for it would be the duty of the boys to receive their garring in complete silence. Failure to do so could disgrace an entire family.

Doereding, was carried away by reminiscences of his own garring.

Much to everyone's amusement, he started singing in a high-pitched voice, imitating an immature child. What he sang I can only describe as a sex song. The tune was both merry and repetitious and the words were crude beyond belief. "*Ciek in tot, ciek in dit, ber wocrodu dei depda. . . .*" ('Young woman, old woman, let the old woman leave our group. . . .') The opening lines set the scene whilst the following ones described making love to young girls; for Doereding had taken an oath at the time of his garring never to miss an opportunity. He described escapades in the reeds, which had caused the cuts on his knees—a mark of Nuer love-making. He sang of a girl called Nyakir, who must have been a childhood sweetheart. Then the words became symbolic bringing laughter from the women gathered around us. "Nyakir, when we meet I shall put red fire in your pipe; I shall give you the red ball when we meet." Doereding sang of buffalo, comparing certain of their habits to those of his girl friend. Then, bringing in a modern touch, he spoke of making love like a bullet from a gun. Turning to me, he invented a verse about the white doctor who injected the tribe with medicine when he should be serving maidens. This latter verse he included in his song, again causing laughter. I was quite content on this moonlit night to sit amongst the Nuer, laughing with them. Becoming bolder with the success of his song Doereding continued with unprintable verses—all references to the sexual act—until tiring of this, he stopped saying that he would return to Gwal Diok to find a girl. So with farewells to all, we set off across the plain.

Travelling at night is always hazardous as the Nuer tend to move swiftly with great sure-footedness. Rial Nyang stumbled around the place, frequently tumbling over sticks in the path which he could not see, despite the light of the moon. I have never got used both to moving at a sort of jog trot at night and being able to see where I was going. My stumbling was a great joke, but they were kind enough to stop from time to time to let me catch up before starting on the next gallop. During the day I could maintain my reputation as a walker and would keep up, or walk ahead, of most Nuer. Sometimes when the sun was at its height, I found my powers of endurance were considerably greater than theirs, especially when it came to carrying heavy loads. This was probably due to the fact that the European diet provides more muscular strength than the Nuer fare. Nevertheless walking at night had given me such an inferiority complex that I once arranged to have a race against most of the ablebodied men in Gwal Diok. To challenge Ethiopians and Sudanese to a running race, when they are well-known as champion marathon runners, might appear absurd, particularly when the challenger was a 38-year-old stockbroker not in the best of trim. My scheme was cunning in that I had noticed that their leg muscles were not particularly well-developed. Therefore, I planned a very short race of 100 yards or less, during which, I correctly guessed, they would not have enough time to get up any speed. Luckily none of the inhabitants of Gwal Diok had been trained in racing starts and they looked on me with amusement as I crouched down digging my toes into a hole ready for the 'off'. Equally, they were surprised and somewhat puzzled when I reached the finishing post before they had begun. Undoubtedly this had done something to redress the balance for my lamentable performance in night trotting.

As we walked back, Doereding joked about the race. I explained how and why I had planned the whole thing, to which he replied that I had the wisdom of an old man. The dogs barked as we approached the huge tree which marked Gwal Diok. When we had beaten them off and made our way through the village, shouting out our names as we passed the various huts so as to be recognized, we headed towards my hut and collapsing onto the ground soon fell into a deep slumber—only occasionally punctuated by the gnawing of rats.

It seemed as though I had hardly dozed off when Kiir and Thiwat woke us saying that the gaar was ready. With frantic haste I gathered together the cameras, film and a bottle of water. Then we all doubled back across the plain towards the other village. I wondered vaguely why I had ever bothered to come back to sleep in Gwal Diok, until I remembered the reason had been to collect my cameras. It was still only five o'clock in the morning when we arrived. As I looked at my light meter I saw that the reading was so low that it would be impossible to film as yet. It was essential for me to try to delay things. Not realizing the danger to the children, I asked Muony to wait until the sun rose higher. He passed this message on to the fathers of the children who accepted the request with resignation but obvious unease. I could not understand why they were in such a hurry, for it seemed to me a shame after I had come all this distance to miss the opportunity of being possibly the first white man to film Nuer garring. Thinking it over afterwards, I saw what tremendous resignation must have been shown on that day by parents and children alike in order to accommodate a stranger. It was all the more remarkable in that the Nuer do not normally allow foreigners to see the head-cutting lest the evil eye should enter and infect the wounds of the children. As we sat and waited, we drank white beer, refreshing despite the fact that I had no breakfast and beer on an empty stomach—above all Nuer beer—can be dangerous. With agonizing slowness the sun appeared whilst minute by minute my light meter recorded better readings.

Just as I was about to give the signal for action, a woman at the far end of the village let out a piercing cry. It sounded like "*O-leay, O-leay, O-leah*" repeated rapidly. This was the call to announce garring. Friends and relations of the family rushed to the spot. From this moment onwards everything happened swiftly.

Two small piles of ashes were made on the ground outside the hut. First one young boy and then another came and lay down on the ground, naked, with arms lightly crossed. Their small bodies covered in white ash looked pathetic as they lay awaiting their fate. Muony sitting out of sight in a corner sharpened a small knife normally kept in a wooden holder. The knife was about 3 inches long, fashioned in the shape of a very small spear with an arrow head. Meanwhile the fathers of the two boys took some ashes and drew a single line down the centre of the foreheads of the children. Muony knelt beside the first child, taking the knife in his right hand and holding the child's head with his left. Starting low down almost by the eyebrow and cutting from the centre of the head, he drove the knife deep into the skull. Six parallel lines were first made on the left hand side. Then he moved across performing the same operation on the right, making sure that the lines were continuous. Blood spurted forth as nerves and blood vessels were cut. If the gaar loses courage or fails to cut deep enough, leaving the nerves partly uncut, the boys would be in terrible pain. One would have thought that the pain would be unbearable anyway, especially when it is realized that the children are given no drugs whatsoever. Moreover, they must prove that they are in complete control of their senses, for when the first cut into the skull is made, the boy shouts out an invocation to assure his father that he will not disgrace the family by being afraid. This is

Muony starts the garring

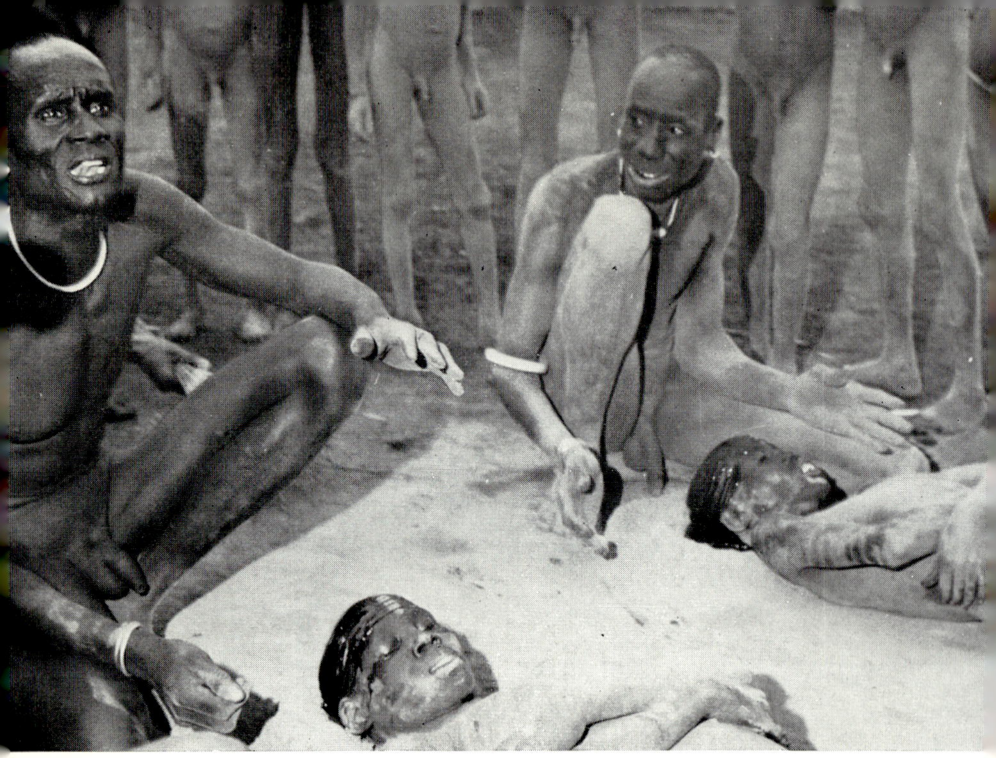

(*above*) Their fathers squat behind the garred boys. (*right*) Flies are kept away

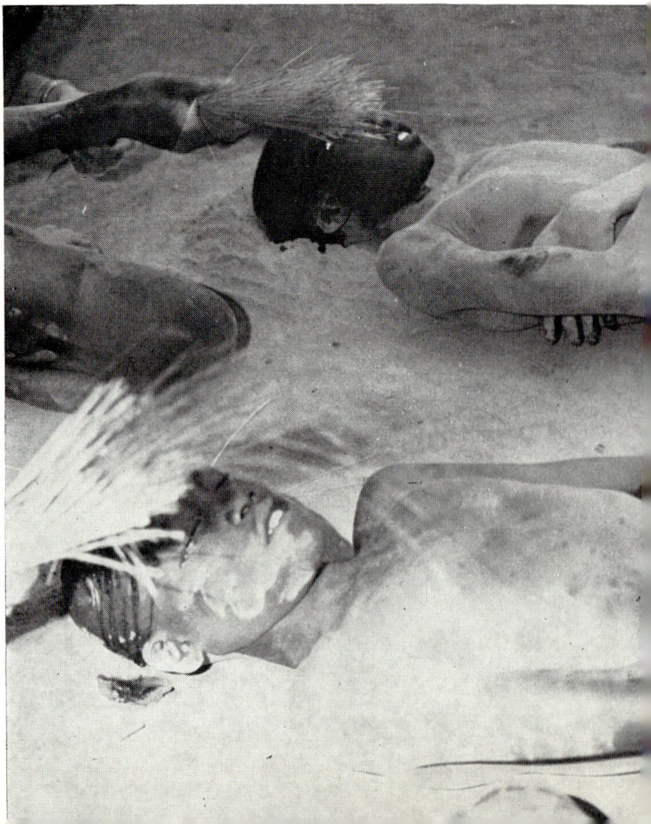

a good example of the ability of man to overcome pain by will-power. An even greater fear than actual pain—namely that of disgracing the family—takes over to conquer normal reactions. Occasionally, Nuer will point to some man or boy and say, "There is one who cried out when he was garred." That unfortunate individual would be shunned by the entire community for the rest of his life.

Once the boys had had their heads cut, the fathers sat over them and waved bunches of straw in the air to keep away the flies. Two other men brought fresh sand to ensure that the blood falling from the heads remained in the pool around them. After ten minutes the flow of blood began to lessen as it congealed. Then took place the most extraordinary example of willpower that I have ever witnessed. The boys, unassisted and obviously weak after their ordeal, summoned all their strength and placing their hands underneath their backs half rose from the ground; keeping their heads tilted backwards they did a sort of crawl towards the nearest hut, maintaining their bodies in a horizontal position. That they were still conscious, let alone able to move, was surprising.

No sooner had two boys completed their ordeal than a cry was heard at the opposite side of the village. Muony went across to start another session. There seemed to be no method of disinfecting the knife between operations, although Muony occasionally cleaned it with sand or sharpened it on a stone. Obviously he was a good gaar and did a really professional job, for the parents congratulated him upon the completion of each operation. Sometimes two boys would be lying side by side. If a number of people were to receive garring in the same row, then the boys would come out one by one, presumably so as not to witness the head-cutting of their neighbours. None of these children moved during the head-cutting and although their arms crossed their small naked bodies, their hands were not even clenched. They appeared totally relaxed. Most boys received only six marks across the forehead but the younger brother who is garred at the same time as his elder brother has a special privilege in store for him in that he receives seven. Why any younger brother should ever be foolish enough to be included in the same session as his elder brother, when by waiting a year or two, he would get away with one less cut, I would not know. I suppose, however, receiving an extra mark is taken as a sign of special courage.

Six boys had by now their heads cut and I had had my fill of this particular spectacle. Feeling queasy in the stomach, partly because of the white beer, I retired into the shade of a hut and drank some water. When Muony had finished he came over to say that he had consulted the 'Spirits Above', Kuoth Nhial, and had been assured that I would bring no harm to the chot. This is the name given to the boys who have received garring during their period of isolation, which lasts approximately a month. For this time they rest allowing their wounds to heal. Most boys told me that during their isolation they had eaten better than they had ever done before in their lives. No one could deny that they had earned this privilege. At any rate I was to be allowed to break the isolation barrier and visit the boys in their seclusion whenever I wished. I thanked Muony, saying that I would come back tomorrow to see how the boys were getting on.

It was two days later before I returned to join Muony in a walk with the children. I was amazed to find how swiftly the wounds had begun to heal. The boys were wearing small leather caps on their heads, sandals on their feet and long cloaks. No part of the body should be open to evil spirits. This period of seclusion also has strange sexual connotations, in that no woman who had taken part in intercourse is allowed near the chot. Another unusual custom for the Nuer is that the children must avoid stepping or walking on cow dung. Nor can they apply the normal cow dung ash which is often used to brush their teeth. The chot carried sticks in their hands to beat off those who approach uninvited, and as we walked they swiped out at any children who came too near.

After a short ramble we all returned to their hut, where two of the boys had been making small mud facsimiles of cows. These they were going to send to their sweethearts; it might well be the beginning of a courtship which would eventually end in marriage. Later they would be called upon by their fathers to take up spears and fight should the village be attacked. After their period of isolation they would no longer eat with their mothers and sisters, but would sit silently at the feet of their fathers to learn about fighting. Each would then be given a spear in recognition of his manhood and a cow or ox would be sacrificed to give him a name, much in the same way as my own sacrifice had ended in my being named Rial Nyang.

We all ate a local form of porridge together—something easy to eat so that the wounds would not re-open through chewing. The boys did not complain of any pain but showed me the Gaar marks under their small leather caps with considerable pride. I was told by Muony that they really should not show these marks to anyone, but because they trusted me as a friend he allowed them to do so. During most of the day we sang songs and they told me about their lives, their aspirations and their hopes. "How wonderful", one boy would say, "no longer to have to milk cows and to have a woman bring you your food." Above all they looked forward to wearing men's jewellery—the huge ivory arm bands made from elephants tusks, the elegant beads which they would put around their waists and the small metal earrings designed in star shapes which Nuer warriors are proud to wear.

Male dances, where women are excluded, are a feature of Nuer life, for they occur at times of preparation for battle. The word for full male status is wutni, and these boys were already longing for the moment when they would emerge to take their place as wutni in Nuer society.

After the period of isolation was over I was able to witness an even more curious ceremony when the entire village lined up to pelt the boys with cow dung. This strange reception indicated that they were now free agents to walk where they liked and act as men. After the agony of the head-cutting, the pelting with cow dung was something of an anti-climax, but the boys loved it. They ran between the cattle whilst both adults and children let fly from all directions. Perhaps since the Nuer have no custard pies to hurl, this particular occasion affords them the opportunity to release any inhibitions which they may have. Nor did the boys being pelted receive this treatment without taking counter-action, for before long I myself had to retreat having received one or two unpleasant missiles on the back and legs. I was only sorry that I would not be able to stay and watch the final ceremonies which would provide these boys with their bull names. There would be singing and dancing and I was sure their girlfriends would be full of admiration. Muony explained that he was going some distance to perform further head-cutting. It would be another year or two before the next age group in this village would be brought forward ready to receive their cuts—that is if the custom continued that long. Already Nuer students returning to their villages after visiting the outside world, are instructing the elders to stop garring for others have told them it is a primitive custom.

A Vulture Overhead

CHAPTER II

Biel wants something,
Biel wants something.
What has to be done?
To provide a cow. . . .
Then Biel will be content.

The garrings were now over and, in the phraseology of the Nuer, 'the knife had been hung up'. I felt as I moved amongst the people of Gwal Diok that I must now look at the men in a new light. Previously the scars on their foreheads had not made much impression on me. Now every Nuer with whom I came in contact seemed a hero. Cattle, initiation, sacrifice and prayer to the spirits—were all part of life. But how did these Nilotic peoples adapt to their environment?

As I looked out of my hut early one morning I saw the usual sights of hut building going on in the distance. Two Nuer men, one of them smoking a pipe, were weaving reeds into the conical shape of a roof. Several others were driving stakes into the ground in a semicircle, weaving reeds in between them and then covering the whole with a coat of mud to make a solid wall. Each part of the house was being made separately and when the roof was completed it was carried to the main structure to be lowered carefully on top. I wondered if it were being built to house a new wife of Gar Quot's since it was on his land.

Kiir arrived with a typical Nuer breakfast, stodgy porridge with an alcoholic flavour. It was just possible to swallow this unappetizing dish so long as I was able to forget that it would have been prepared in gourd previously disinfected with human urine. As a special treat Kiir had brought me some green oil to pour over the porridge. It was made out of butter with herbs added but the taste was even more disgusting than that of the porridge on its own. As Kiir sat on the ground in front of me with his eyes raised in adoration, there was nothing else to do except gulp down the dish with all the pretence of enjoyment which hypocrisy would allow.

Many cattle were lowing in the distance. One or two women sat milking cows. There is an extraordinary custom amongst the Nuer whereby the women blow into the vaginas of the cows to make the supply of milk more abundant. I know of no other peoples in Africa who practice this, but it may well be that it is common amongst other pastoral tribes. The children were playing nearby with the usual shrieks accompanying the game of make-believe spearing. Young warriors-to-be were throwing their pointed sticks at a target swung around in the air on the end of a piece of string. It always amazed me, how the man in the middle in charge of the swinging target, managed to escape being struck by numerous pointed sticks. Perhaps these children's instinct of survival is so well developed that it influences their reflexes even at this early age. Certainly the only time I tried to swing the target, I succeeded in getting struck both in the foot and on the backside! Perhaps in my case it was intentional, in revenge for some unpleasant penicillin jabs.

On this particular day Thiwat did not turn up as usual. Later he explained to me that he had been conducting negotiations for his forthcoming marriage (see Chapter 13). It had come as a complete surprise to me that he was even thinking of getting married. Doereding was suffering from an attack of malaria, sometimes feverish, at others just exhausted. I would have the day to myself.

After sick parade, which brought the normal number of incurable patients, I settled down to examine some of the people in the village. Across from my hut was a crazy old man with grey hair, given to constant muttering. He was accepted by everyone in the village. He would wander over, take a look at me, say something, scream, charge about, then return to his hut quite peacefully. Everyone laughed, but people treated him with a kindness which is not known in our society. It was thought that he had suffered a divine misfortune so the villagers helped him. (We lock up our insane in mental homes, where, to judge by newspaper reports, they are not always treated with the kindness they deserve. They are separated from their families, perhaps the only people who can really assist them.) Nor does this type of insanity automatically debar someone from doing normal work. The old man opposite for instance, either tended the cattle or at other times helped the women harvesting corn or carrying burdens.

I had been talking to Doereding, as he lay on the ground beside me, about this acceptance of madness as a natural phenomenon when we noticed the old man heading off to work with the women.

This prompted Doereding despite his sickness to tell me a story which completely contradicted all that I had thought and learnt so far about Nuer homosexual relations. It had always been stressed by the tribesmen that homosexuality between men was impossible, for if discovered amongst them it could be punishable by death. Doereding now told me about a crazy man he had once known who lived near Nasir in the Sudan and who frequently dressed as a woman. This was different Doereding explained, because "the man had actually become a woman"; the prophet of Deng had been consulted and had agreed to his change of status. The prophet had decided to call on the spirits and after consultation had declared that indeed the man was a woman. Therefore he could dress in women's clothes and behave as a woman. From that time onwards it was agreed that 'he' should be called 'she', and 'she' was also allowed to marry a husband. All very confusing, and so totally against what the Nuer had been telling me, that I questioned Doereding carefully, but this failed to produce any further explanation. Perhaps this goes to show how easily the people will accept the ruling of a prophet, or again how easily their own rules can be changed should the gods be willing.

Under the main tree in Gwal Diok, Gar Quot sat playing the tom, a Nuer violin, humming the tunes composed by his ancestors. He looked peaceful enough as he sat there surrounded by the elders, yet the words he sang related to blood-thirsty battles between the tribes. Nearby, two or three men were twisting rope. Others were cutting tethering pegs to use as stakes for stretching skins.

For a few moments the rain pelted down, but these heavy showers only lasted ten minutes at the most, then the clouds blew by overhead. Crab apples had fallen from the tree under the force of the rain and were hastily collected by the children, who bit into them only to make faces at the sourness of the fruit. Two women came with gourds to scoop up water from the puddles. Kiir left my side to perform an act of charity for one of our neighbours. He was going give a young girl of 12 or 13 a haircut. It was a pretty brutal affair for several times the sharp instrument he was using, a type of home-make scissors, slipped and cut into her head, but she didn't seem to mind. At any rate it was a change to see Kiir joining in village life and for once enjoying himself.

A sick calf was being given a drink of water by two young tribesmen. One held the struggling animal while the other forced its mouth open and poured the contents of a small gourd down its throat. This reminded me yet again of the great affection felt by these people for their cattle. Nuer folklore relates how once upon a time there was a huge conference held for all the 'Spirits Above' and all 'The Spirits of the Earth', including man. Man was praised for his outstanding contribution to the world, but requested the spirits to raise him above the status of the animals. The 'Spirits of Above' agreed but did not want man to suffer loneliness so they decreed that wherever he went cattle were to follow. In this way man would be rewarded with milk and meat, so as to ensure his survival. But a stern warning was given not to abuse this privilege, for cattle were only to be killed when the spirits allowed or demanded it. The Nuer were to be permitted meat through sacrifice, but not by means of direct slaughter. The difference was subtle but remains all important to this day.

Not all of the 'just-so' stories are so relevant to everyday life as that of 'man and cattle', but many have a charm all of their own. Take the story of the elephant and the frog. The two animals had a bitter argument and the frog, who had been gravely insulted, declared he would kill the elephant. How was this to be done? In the cool of the evening the frog lay waiting for the elephant at the water-hole where he usually came to drink. When the elephant sucked up the water from the pool the frog was also drawn into his trunk. There he blocked the passage and set up such a din croaking and chirping that the elephant lost his head completely and began beating his trunk against a nearby tree, to get rid of the irritation. The frog got a few bruises in the process but the elephant damaged his trunk so badly that he could no longer use it for eating or drinking. And so the elephant died.

Another Nuer story came to mind. The 'Spirits Above' used to favour each animal in turn, particularly the monkey, who was allowed to walk upright amongst them. The monkey enjoyed this position, but being boastful and proud grew more arrogant as time went by. The spirits were soon irritated, as were all the other animals, including man. One day the monkey went too far by insulting everyone and throwing things at them. So the 'Spirits Above' cursed the monkey, saying that from that day forth he should walk on four legs instead of two. Nor was that the end of his humiliation, for now the monkey's red bottom was plainly visible to all. So ashamed was he of this that he ran off into the forest and from then onwards lived in the trees.

As soon as the men returned from work that evening I called Kiir and asked him to cook some of our meat. It was not a good time to eat because I was surrounded by people and the Nuer consider it ill-mannered to eat in public, but I was hungry. Several men had come to sing into the tape recorder those long songs describing their heroic exploits which so delighted them. I would first record one man so as not to hurt his feelings. He would burst forth in a loud wail, either describing the saga of his battles or listing his female conquests. The surrounding men would join in the chorus but the periodic loud shrieks of the singer were to me agonizing noises which made the control needle of my tape recorder leap over the maximum noise indicator. As the weird cries were heard throughout Gwal Diok, Kiir reappeared embarrassed at having had to cook for me in front of the other men. I felt guilty at having asked him to do so. Normally he performed his services quietly in the evenings so that as few people as possible would realize that he was doing a woman's work.

I sat cross-legged on the ground and started to eat my meal, watching all that was going on around me. As I did so something must have caught my attention for at one point I held aloft a piece of meat in my right hand and paused before eating it. There was a sudden gust of wind. A sharp pain came from my forefinger. A trickle of blood ran down my wrist. The meat was gone. A vulture had swooped down and removed my meal. For a moment my first thought was the loss of the food, though Kiir soon managed to produce more, but then I wondered if the claws of vultures were poisonous. After bathing my hand in Dettol and applying a bandage from out of my medical box to what was really only a small scratch, I settled down once again to the evening meal. But now I noticed a look of admiration amongst those sitting around the hut. Contact with birds, even vultures, is always thought to mean —some manifestation of the divine. The fact that a vulture had descended and eaten from my hand was yet another sign that Rial Nyang was in league with the spirits.

Dancing is Dangerous

CHAPTER 12

Young woman, old woman—
Let the old woman leave our group—
Young woman, come, come.
(Nuer Love Song.)

Doereding had frequently sung this love song. Whenever he did he had been surrounded by the girls of Gwal Diok laughing and giggling in embarrassment. Often these songs had become excessively crude but they never ceased to delight the audience. Strangest of all was when I once heard a group of girls praying for a cloudy night,—but not so cloudy that it would actually rain. They had asked that it should be "quite dark" so that they could get away from their homes without being seen by their brothers or relations—an unusual subject for prayer.

Kor Jum had in spite of the smallpox outbreak in some of the neighbouring villages, promised a day dance in the village of Wiu. In the early morning twin drums had been brought out in a number of villages and attached to stakes driven deep into the earth. From time to time youths would beat on these drums so that the whole area would know that a dance or *boula* was about to take place. Recently the smallpox epidemic which had swept across the territories of the eastern Nuer had led to the banning of day dances, although for some reason Kor Jum previously considered that night dances did not involve any risk of spreading the disease. This dance was therefore to be an exception to the general rule banning day dances. Despite Kor Jum's original assurances that a day dance was under way, it became increasingly apparent that no one would be there on time. Twice the dance almost started—a few people had come, but seeing that the party was not under way, had drifted off again. It seemed as though the dance was unlikely to take place at all, so somewhat disheartened I returned from Wiu to Gwal Diok after waiting at the prophet's village most of the day.

The sun had now set; I had just settled down to a comfortable meal cooked by the faithful Kiir when runners arrived to say that the dance had begun. Simultaneously drums were beating all over the plain. Groups of Nuer youths with painted white faces, and spears in their right hands, came charging into the villages displaying themselves in all their manhood to admiring females. This was the method of inviting the girls to dance. The men came in groups of ten to twenty, all in one long line, leaping, jumping, and screaming—some of them with their entire bodies painted white—others with feathers in their hair—some carried rifles instead of spears, a few wore leopard skins but most were in torn shorts, specially saved up for these occasions, or else wore nothing at all. The girls ran screaming into their huts but I suppose this was only out of modesty or perhaps in order to prepare to make themselves more beautiful. When they emerged the younger women wore nothing on top but had put on brief skirts of dangling leather strips decorated with beads, like the grass skirts associated with Hawaii. As the men charged from village to village rounding up the girls, Doereding and I made our way back again to Wiu.

Kor Jum welcomed me with great ceremony and together we sat on a goatskin placed on the ground under a large tree in front of the temple of Wiu. Two sets of twin drums were being beaten and about two hundred tribesmen were already dancing. The stamping of their feet raised a cloud of dust so that it became difficult to see or breathe. Whereas the drums beat rhythmically, the dancing appeared to have no general pattern. Men whirled around in small circles singing or shouting completely different songs or slogans.

It was not long before a party of naked warriors from Gwal Diok all about 16 to 18 years old, descended on me and dragged me into the centre of the dance so that I found myself thrust between the sweating bodies of charging Nuer. The light was fading but there were still no girls on the scene. We simply dashed about shouting what sounded to me like "*Yeah l'attack aboujak*". Occasionally we clashed with other groups, and I would find myself hurled forward with resounding force towards advancing tribesmen. I would crash into them (since the linked arms of one's comrades allowed little freedom of movement), and then recoil somewhat shaken, certainly bruised, and sometimes even cut. It was rather like being used as a battering ram.

I managed to tear myself away, sweating and exhausted to return to Kor Jum. The wise old prophet was hidden behind a tree, and together we drank a considerable amount of refreshing distilled corn whisky. But, alas, my trials and tribulations were not over, for Kor Jum decided that I had done so well in the initial dancing, that it was time I did a turn with him as my teacher. Grasping me with one arm, and shoving a spear into my right hand, he dragged me forward into the centre of the *mêlée*. The drummers increased the tempo; the tribesmen, to my horror, ceased dancing and formed a large circle leaving Kor Jum and myself in the centre. There were shouts of "Kor Jum" and "Rial Nyang" as I gazed about stupefied. The cloud of dust gradually settled. Only the moon now gave us any light, for night had fallen. Kor Jum ordered leopard skins to be brought and these were then slung over us in the manner of a toga or cloak. I hung back hoping that all I had to do was watch, but I was pushed forward by the tribesmen who were not going to let me off so easily. By now there were also giggles from the girls who had arrived to see the star performance. Never in my life have I so wanted to crawl away ignominiously and hide.

First slowly, and then with increasing speed, Kor Jum began to twist, squirm and undulate to the music. His spear formed an extension of his right arm as he held it high in the air or charged about with it in a horizontal position. Sometimes the upper half of his body swayed as if it were disengaged from the lower half. At other moments he would leap into the air and land crouched on the ground hissing and growling. Each time I retreated from him, I was prodded (sometimes none too gently) by the encircling tribesmen. There was nothing for it; I had to dance. With a Nuer screech I entered the fray, wearing my leopard skin and holding a splendid spear above my head. I tried to imitate every movement or action of the prophet. As he leapt and hissed and spat, so I followed a second later. If he charged in my direction, I charged in his, managing to stop at the last moment in order to avoid collision. The drummers, intoxicated with the scene, increased the tempo of their drumming. Faster and faster we danced, higher and higher we leapt while the crowds shouted with delight. At first I thought the Nuer were just being polite, for I was certain that my leaping about would be ridiculous in their eyes. Perhaps it was, but if so, they managed to hide their scorn remarkably well. At any rate every time Kor Jum and I tried to stop, the crowds shoved us forward again. For well over an hour the two of us danced opposite each other until, exhausted, we both fell to the ground. One or two tribesmen brought aragy and white beer as a reward for our efforts. We consumed it in private.

Originally one of my objectives had been to film a Nuer day dance, but when night had fallen and I had no lights, I had to abandon my photographic ambitions. My other intention had been to make tape recordings of the music. Since every limb and muscle was now suffering from exhaustion, it seemed to me a suitable time to switch from dancing to tape-recording. Alas, popularity can sometimes lead to frustration, for each time the tape recorder was started crowds of Nuer would crush in upon me. "Rial Nyang" was repeated whenever I appeared. The microphone of my tape-recorder had this interesting message shouted into it over and over again.

Somehow the fact that it was night, that the drums were going and that I had been dancing amongst them, had all helped to overcome the shyness of the girls who now surrounded me. Sometimes lines of dancing women would advance and then retreat, flicking their bottoms upwards in a provocative manner so that their leather skirts undulated. This art of bottom flicking is a particular skill of Nuer girls. One of the most amusing sights is to see the young girls of about 6 or 7 years old practising as hard as they can. At this age bottoms hardly move but after years of muscular practice they flick their bottoms to great effect.

After about half an hour of unsuccessful recording of the various tumultuous and disorganized noises which accompanied the general dancing, I found myself being dragged forward once again into the throng. This time it was Doereding who led me. Kor Jum joined us and said he would find us some girls. This was a particular privilege since the prophet had the authority to choose any of the girls he wished. We selected a group of the most attractive, though to my mind they were all a little young—probably between the ages of 12 to 15, but of course after that age I remembered they are generally married. We danced in a line opposite them but now there was some point to our movements. I soon learnt the art of carrying ones spear in the right hand and following the movement of the girls bottoms. One should never get near enough to actually spear them—this would be considered the height of ill manners. But the whole time one had to pretend that this was the real objective. When the girls advanced we retreated, when they retreated we advanced. All the time I shouted the one song I had learnt, "*Yeah l'attack aboujak*".

Seeing Kiir standing gloomily on the edge of the circle I grabbed him forcing him to take the prophet's place, for Kor Jum having found us girls had retired. Kiir was delighted; he had not danced all evening. I shall always remember the happiness registered in his smile when I pulled him forward in to the middle of that dance.

Time had long since ceased to matter to me; exhaustion had become the order of the night. One difficult manoeuvre, which I could never have accomplished on my own, was that of remaining dancing opposite my partner, or her bottom! It sounds simple enough but what in fact happened was that each time a sequence of drumming ended the girls with linked arms would weave their way in and out of the crowd. When the drums started again their partners were supposed to be dancing opposite them as before. This was easy for the Nuer, but when I attempted it on my own, I found I got hopelessly lost and never arrived dancing opposite the same girl twice. Nor could I recognize the girls in the darkness, but with the help of Kiir and Doereding we somehow arrived in the right place at the right time. Once or twice the girls tired of their companions. They would drift away leaving the men dancing on their own.

Several times I found Gar Quot dancing near me with groups of elder men or chieftains, but on the whole, with the exception of my dances with Kor Jum, it was expected that I would remain with the younger age group. No sooner had I collapsed from dancing with Doereding and Kiir than this group of young bloods appeared again and whisked me to my feet, only to start charging and dashing about all over again. It seemed as if the dancing would never stop, for whereas initially there had been some excitement for me in watching the movements and gyrations, now after several hours the whole thing was becoming rather tedious, certainly very hot and dusty. There must now have been nearly a thousand Nuer swarming about. The drums beat louder and louder accompanied by an occasional blast from what sounded like a military bugle. At about midnight I fell on to the ground beneath a large tree in front of the temple of Wiu. This was where the evening had started. As far as I was concerned this was where it was going to finish.

Strange as it may seem I was allowed a few minutes rest, almost dozing off despite the noise and dust, when a group of girls arrived chattering and shouting, "Rial Nyang". Something was about to happen for they tugged at my hands and leopard skin, indicating that I should follow. I thought that there was something to be seen—perhaps a small animal or a house where more refreshment would be offered. Anything would be better than the dust and

(*above*) Muony with the boys garred three days before

(*below*) On the way to the dance at Wiu

(*above*) Children preparing stick spears for games

(*below*) Washing in the Baro River

noise of the dance. I felt flattered that for the first time the girls were beginning to take an interest in a stranger. Gradually it became apparent that I was not moving entirely under my own steam, girls were pulling my hands from the front, others were shoving from behind. I was being propelled rapidly into a rather muddy marsh. For one horrible moment I wondered if it was their intention to take me to some isolated spot and push my head under water. Certainly everyone seemed eager that I should hurry.

Next to my utter amazement amidst screeches of "Rial Nyang" I was knocked to the ground and what I can only describe as a rugger scrum took place on top of me. About a dozen girls screeching and clawing were tearing me to pieces. Nails dug into my flesh. I thought there would be no possibility of rescue. There was no point in shouting although the pain was beginning to become unbearable as the cuts and scratches increased. I fought as vigorously as I could but the odds were overwhelming. There was no clothing left on me as my leopard skin had been torn off. Just at that moment the prophet Kor Jum must have arrived for the girls were removed from on top of me. Grabbing the girls by the scruff of their necks, he had flung them aside. Some got cracks across the face, others were kicked or pushed away until Kor Jum stood protectively over me. Gathering what was left of me and my pride, I struggled to my feet. Together with Kor Jum I marched off, the leopard skin back around my shoulders, the spear reinstated in my right hand. As we left Kor Jum turned to a few of the remaining girls still stunned from his attack, and with great dignity declared that Rial Nyang was not to be assaulted according to the custom of Nuer. "Rial Nyang", he said, "has not come to steal our women like other foreigners but to bring peace and medicine to the followers of Wiu." Rape had been avoided!

CHAPTER 13

Thiwat gets Married by Hire Purchase

> Let it be cloudy but let it not rain.
> Let the evening darken, so that our maidens
> May pass to the huts of their lovers in silence.

Although Rial Nyang may thankfully have been excluded from final integration into the social life of Gwal Diok, for he remained a bachelor, Thiwat was not intending to follow the same course. It will be remembered one day he had calmly appeared at the door of my hut announcing that he would be unable to help me for the next forty-eight hours. I had been planning a trip across the marshes to Coitung, where the prophet of Deng lived and was therefore aggrieved with Thiwat for deserting me at such short notice. However since he announced his intention of getting married tomorrow, I could only offer him congratulations. You would have thought that any individual about enter so soon into the state of matrimony would have shown some form of excitement or anticipation—some might even have shown reluctance—but Thiwat talked of marriage much in the same way as one might discuss having lunch or going fishing. It is only when I realized what a long-drawn-out affair Nuer marriage is, that I could understand this attitude.

To go back to the early days of Nuer youth, one of the first signs of attention to the opposite sex is shown at the time of garring. It is then that the boys compose love songs as well as sending small clay figures of cows to their girl friends via an intermediary. Until the time of garring any advances the boys might make would be disregarded as being merely the stupidity of children. After garring the children have become men and have to be taken seriously. If the parents of a particular girl disapprove of the attentions of any of her boyfriends they will make it absolutely plain by forbidding their daughter to have anything further to do with the boy in question. It will then become the duty of the brothers of the girl, if there are any, or in their absence other male relations, to ensure that parental rule is obeyed. Many were the times during my visit that I have seen girls grabbed by their brothers and dragged away from a dance because they were thought to be flirting with men who were in some way unsuitable either by wealth, reputation or consanguinity. As has been seen my habit of roaming from village to village might have led some to suppose that I was in search of a Nuer wife, but the prophet had now explained the position.

Before the unfortunate occasion of my near rape on the dance floor, I had indeed been followed from village to village by one hideously ugly old lady. This witch-like character with a hunchback, a hollow and haggard face with little flesh clinging to her bones, must have been in her late fifties or early sixties. At first I thought she followed me merely to obtain medicine but later I discovered that she was also something of a wit. Just as I would be setting up my travelling clinic in a village, this old trout would start addressing the crowd, causing them to laugh. Doereding, Thiwat and others would join in, but no one would tell me what it was all about. One day when the old girl was excelling herself, pointing at me and shouting whilst declaiming to the crowd, I asked Doereding to give me a full translation. What she said was as follows: "Rial Nyang knows that I am old, ugly and have long since lost my husband. There is now no one to look after me, but I am not demanding. For a husband I would fetch water, cook meals and keep the house in order. I would not need much in the way of clothes for I have little vanity left but would be content with an old hide to keep me warm at night. Now Rial Nyang may find me ugly in the full light of day but why does he not try me at night? Would he then notice what I looked like, and could he not then appreciate the kindness I should offer? Because I am old and ugly I will forget that he had no garring, that he is of a strange colour and that he does not belong to us. Is this, truly, not a bargain and the basis for a suitable marriage?"

On hearing this translation I was horrified to find that Doereding and the others had let this go so far. I begged them to tell the old girl that she had not got a chance for I already had hundreds of prospective wives in England. Such a lie was not acceptable, even in jest and so there seemed to me only one solution left: that was to declare in public that I greatly appreciated the qualities of this faithful old girl who had followed me everywhere, but that, according to Nuer law, I was still a child. True, I had wrinkles on my forehead, but these were not enough. As a child I could not marry, and she would do better to choose a more worthy Nuer. I was certain that all of the men present would be able to appreciate her qualities. In this way, what could have turned out to be an embarrassing situation, was dealt with in what I hoped turned out to be a diplomatic manner, without offending anyone's feelings or honour.

What is difficult for the European to understand is how long and drawn out the whole process of Nuer marriage is. Thiwat had certainly known his wife-to-be for the last ten years. Undoubtedly he had had other girlfriends, flirtations and perhaps even children born out of wedlock; certainly he was no innocent for being the son of Gar Quot had given him many advantages in life. On the other hand, some form of fidelity would be required of him from the moment that he had paid an engagement deposit. The first step in Nuer marriage, arising out of courtship, is the deposit. When this is being put down all the relatives of both sides gather together to examine the heredity of the man involved, since it is essential to prove that in no circumstances could incest be charged. For any family which has been accused of incest is considered unclean and the children of such a family are punished by the spirits. Marriage itself is for the procreation of children, and should these not appear the woman is nearly always accused of being the culpable party. Should she remain barren for a number of years, she will often be returned to her parents, who in turn will be required to hand back the dowry.

In order to gather sufficient cattle to pay the initial deposit, Thiwat might have gone on a raid or else borrowed as many cattle as he could from his richer relatives. Today he had decided that there were enough cattle to undertake the second part of his marriage, but two years before this he had taken four cows and one ox, leaving them with the parents of his bride to be. He had then entered into a relationship known as yoat or nung gok. In other words, he had taken the cattle to the bride's home and declared his intention of eventually marrying the girl. On that occasion, Thiwat told me, he had taken three of his best friends to the girl's home where they had danced throughout the night. The friends of the groom-to-be are always treated with great respect, although, by tradition, they do not eat near, or in the presence of, the future in-laws. For two days Thiwat and his friends hung around the bride's house until finally they had made themselves known in the area. Thiwat's colleagues had also formed some useful associations of another nature.

All of this had happened some time ago, but now the biggest and most important part of the marriage was to take place, the ngut. As I was to discover, probably the most difficult episode in the ngut is the bargaining over the cattle which are eventually to be exchanged for the bride. I was fully prepared for the whole evening to belong to the groom, but was surprised to find that the wedding has very little to do with either of the youngsters. They are merely the pawns in an enormously complicated game of social relationships. The really important people are the relatives on both sides, for they are the ones who enter into endless arguments about the cattle, including the qualities of each individual beast. Negotiators are specially chosen by each side for their power of almost continuous speech, with the object of boring and exhausting the opponents in the hope that after hours of argument someone will be so sick of the subject that they will give way.

The first thing that happened in Gwal Diok was that a few old ladies leapt about letting out weird shrieks outside Thiwat's hut. Then accompanied by Thiwat and some of his friends, they arrived in the centre of the village. Everyone seemed in merry spirits when I was asked to join the party. Thiwat and his friends were wearing leopard skins. One older woman, who must have been a relation of Thiwat's, had an absurd hat on her head from under which hideous swollen ear lobes dangled. Some form of growth had attached itself to both ears—but despite her deformity she lead all the singing and dancing, prancing around and truly entering into the spirit of a wedding. Thiwat's female relations, dressed also in their skins, swayed and undulated in front of the huts of others. This was sort of an announcement of the wedding. The boys lept into the air hissing and shouting or simply making raucous noises. The drums were placed in the middle of the village. As the day went by, more and more people gathered joining in the dancing. The groom is supposed to sing some of his favourite songs, but if Thiwat thought that anyone was going to listen to him, he was greatly mistaken. All of the dancers were intent on their own gyrations.

Food had been brought in large quantities, white beer in particular. The serious side of the wedding was taking place at a short distance from the dancing, beneath the main tree. There Gar Quot, his friends and relations were seated in a long row, some twenty men in all. Opposite them sat twenty of the girl's family. The two groups were aligned with only about 3 feet between them as they faced each other. A quantity of small sticks were placed in the middle and one by one, accompanied by endless discussion, these sticks were moved in patterns from one side to the other. This was the cattle discussion or negotiation. Depending on the outcome of this particular session, it would be decided whether or not Thiwat was accepted as a suitable husband for the girl.

During the dance the behaviour of the bride must be one of assumed reluctance. Even were she madly in love, she must pretend to have no interest in the man in question. The object is to establish an atmosphere whereby the parents of the bride can truly say that their daughter is reluctant to marry, thereby extracting an even greater number of cattle. There are a number of occasions when the ngut temporarily breaks up because the two parties have not been able to agree on the bridal price. Sometimes, I was told, the price has been settled beforehand when the first deposit is paid, but even then, if one or two years have elapsed, the cattle may have changed in health or size. There is also the matter of deciding the fate of any calves that may have been born of these animals. Substitutes may be demanded and certain of the cattle will be inspected by suspicious relatives fearing that the other side are trying to palm off on them unworthy beasts.

Being an 'eager-beaver' to assimilate everything I could relating to Nuer customs, I rushed about on the one hand watching the negotiations of the relatives and on the other the younger folk dancing. Thiwat showed no apparent interest in his bride to be. Perhaps it was only to irritate or inflame her with passion, that he followed or flirted with nearly all the other girls present! Meanwhile these maidens concentrated on their provocative dancing, namely bottom-flicking, with the men often following them, spears or guns grasped in their right hands, letting out occasional yelps of admiration of simulated bravery.

Dancing and feasting continued well into the night, and after approximately five hours both sides announced that an agreement had been reached. I fully expected Thiwat and his bride to disappear off together on a long honeymoon, but as I was sitting with Gar Quot and Doereding they explained that the ngut is only the middle marriage ceremony; there is still the third and final part which has to take place, namely the muot. It is not possible to lay down the precise number of cattle which are handed over at any given moment, but if we estimate that approximately four or five change hands at the time of the engagement, another ten to twelve might change hands subsequently at the ngut. The total could then be brought up to twenty or twenty-five at the time of the muot.

The muot represents the final instalment and, indeed, until this has been paid the girl is still not the absolute possession of the husband. Should the groom have difficulty in finding the necessary cattle, he may have to wait as long as four years between the two ceremonies. For two to three days during the muot the bride's girl friends enjoy themselves in the groom's village, but finally the time comes to return home and the girl is at last left alone with her husband to take up residence in the new surroundings acting as a proper wife, cooking, carrying water and growing crops in the fields.

Doereding told me that Thiwat would not have long to wait. He might even collect the girl within six months, but there was no possibility of disappearing off with her tonight! He might on some subsequent occasion sneak off secretly, for doubtless he had slept with her before, but on public occasions it is essential for the groom to behave with impeccable probity. So in many ways the final wedding dances are something of a bore for the bride and groom. Nevertheless the whole affair gave endless opportunities for the relations to squabble amongst themselves and provided even better opportunities for friends of the bride and groom to make love with new partners. I have said little of my impression of the girl whom Thiwat was going to marry for the very good reason that she remained almost continuously in the background. She did not seem anything very special in the way of looks. Nor could I approach her myself without causing comment. So alas I never found out if Thiwat had made a good choice.

In Nuer society the wife will be lucky to remain the sole recipient of her husband's affections. Thiwat, for instance, whilst only really three-quarters of the way through obtaining his first wife, already had plans for a second. Knowing him, I am sure that if in a few years' time I were to return to Gwal Diok, I would find his collection growing rapidly. The normal Nuer system is for a warrior, once he has accumulated wealth, to purchase anything up to three or four wives, not all at once, but perhaps one every five years. In this way the man can enjoy the affections and care of a mature woman while retaining the right every now and then to select a more attractive or younger addition to the household. The women seem to get on quite well together, for few Nuer warriors would dare to take a young wife disapproved of by his earlier consorts—life would simply not be worth living.

Soon Thiwat would be building himself another house and the semi-circle around his present dwelling would extend to provide a series of similar huts, reserved for each of his wives. He might then visit them in turn, depending on their state of health and pregnancies, but a wife who kept a good home and cooked a good meal would have the best chance of retaining his affections. This, however, was looking far ahead.

Return to Civilization

CHAPTER 14

Today our courage has changed our luck.
Have not a low opinion of us
Our success depends on Wiu
And Wiu will back our case.

It was four o'clock in the morning and Gwal Diok was sound asleep—insofar as a native village can ever be said to be asleep. There are still noises—the rustling of cattle, the occasional cough or a tribesman talking in his sleep. From the time to time a dog might yelp, for no other reason than that a cow had inadvertently trodden on it—the poor animal would continue whimpering in pain. Then there were noises inside the hut. The night rummaging of the rats sounded to a weary would-be sleeper like an army battalion on the move. My dreams had taken me back to the days spent with my regiment with trucks on army manoeuvres rumbling across the Egyptian desert.

Suddenly I woke to discover my dream had become a reality and that two vehicles were in fact moving across the plain. Gwal Diok was soon awake and in a panic. Tribesmen grabbed their spears or guns—the women screamed inside their huts. This could only mean trouble—it might be some Sudanese army vehicles which had strayed across the border, or more likely the Ethiopian police on a punitive raid. At any rate, the men were not going to be caught napping! They charged across the plain in ever increasing numbers towards the oncoming vehicles. Still the trucks advanced making for Gwal Diok—weaving about to avoid ditches or swamps but continuing in the same general direction.

When finally a party of some five hundred Nuer arrived, there was no doubt that the trucks and their occupants were virtually captives. It was still night, but I could see a white man jump down from the leading vehicle. I marvelled how he had managed to cross such difficult country with his vehicles. It must certainly be the first time trucks had reached Gwal Diok! The man advanced towards me flinging his arms around my shoulders. It was Thomas Mattanovitch, my white hunter, and his team, just one month late to the day. "Thank God you are alive," he muttered dramatically, and I made a similar response. Admittedly, it would probably be more serious for a white hunter to lose his client, than for a client to lose his white hunter—in the eyes of the law. Thomas's crew, plus his cook, Berthe, dismounted from the vehicles but the Nuer stood around glowering. Their sleep had been interrupted by these strangers, a white man, two Anuak boys and two Amhara, one of them a woman, to make matters worse. A bleary eyed Gar Quot stepped forward, "Tell them to go away, Rial Nyang before trouble starts. These may be friends of yours, but there are Anuak amongst them whom my men would gladly kill. You are welcome in this village but not these foreigners. Get them out quickly for their own safety."

If I had been becoming complacent in Nuer society, and relying too much on their friendship, this would have brought me sharply back to reality. These recently acquired friends of mine were a fighting people, whose memory is often short and whose mood can change in an instant. There was no doubt that the present mood was ugly, for Gar Quot meant every word he said. Thomas and his crew were in danger. For some time I had been wondering what I should do in the unlikely event of Thomas turning up, but I never thought I should have to send him away again. I had forgotten that he employed Anuak and spoke their language. No wonder the Nuer looked on him with suspicion. Berthe, Thomas's cook had first inspected my hut, then the Nuer, and letting out an Amharic oath, declared I had gone native. I was wearing a pair of underpants in honour of the visitors. Some iron bracelets were to be seen on my wrists and ankles, and my hair and beard were an unruly mess. For some reason I had also clasped a spear in my right hand when attack seemed certain, and I was still holding it when they arrived. My revolver would have been more to the point, but, like the Nuer, I had grabbed the nearest weapon. Thomas had arrived just in time to stop me turning completely Nuer. Nevertheless, I truly resented this intrusion. Perhaps it was because my time with the Nuer was nearly over. It was too early yet for me to fully understand that Rial Nyang's friends had cast a shadow of suspicion over him. Previously, I had been trusted by all—but for the next couple of days whilst Thomas remained in the area, I noticed a change taking place. When I moved out of Gwal Diok the sick still came for treatment, and the occasional tribesman still called out Rial Nyang, but the girls no longer giggled and pointed at me and the friendly smiles left some faces. Thiwat and Kiir no longer turned up to help, although Gar Quot and Kor Jum both visited me after I moved from Gwal Diok to Thomas's camp.

That night it did not take Thomas and his men long to realize they were unwanted. Sadly they remounted the trucks and together with a Nuer escort, were shown a route across the plains towards the Baro river. There they pitched camp in the early hours of the morning—still in Nuer country, but nearer to an Ethiopian police post and an Anuak village. Later that morning, and after a few hours sleep, I too left Gwal Diok in the manner of the locals. There were no goodbyes. I simply picked up my few possessions and walked away. I felt too sad to say formal farewells and anyway it seemed more appropriate to leave quietly. Doereding kept looking back at Gwal Diok as we walked across the plain; after all, it had been our home for several weeks.

The camp by the river lacked nothing for comfort; three tents, one with a mosquito-proof verandah, chairs, tables, a transistor radio, tins of food, eggs and newly baked bread, camp beds to sleep on and even a canvas shower which was hung up in a tree. It was an ideal site, Berthe was a good cook and Thomas' team was well-trained. I should have appreciated the cool beer out of his refrigerator and the chance to get clean and tidy, more than I did. Instead I was already feeling homesick for Gwal Diok, although illogically I did not want to go back there, for Thomas was someone to talk to. He told me of his frantic efforts to reach me, the strange messages he had received from runners about my being with the Nuer, and one story had even indicated that I had joined the Anya-Nya. Once his vehicles had been repaired, he had made his way back to Gambela, and from there had come with all speed to Teleuth. He was bitterly disappointed at having missed a safari and explained that he could not possibly charge me anything for my two days in his camp. The return trip was also to be free in compensation for the inconvenience caused. Nothing could be fairer than that! Previously, I had thought of a thousand tortures I would apply to Thomas for not turning up; now I could only feel sorry that he had lost money on my account by missing a 'safari'.

Gar Quot came several times to our camp by the river during the next two days—after all, it was only a few miles away from Gwal Diok. He would sit staring at me whilst occupying the best chair, occasionally clapping his hands for a bottle of European beer. Berthe decidedly did not take to the Nuer. She was a woman of great character and beauty, but she frequently let fly at the tribesmen, either kicking them out of camp or cursing them for standing in her way. To be so treated by a woman was an insult. It was lucky that our camp in that area did not last any longer than it did. The Nuer were acting with restraint. They would willingly have chopped Berthe to pieces for the wounding insults she hurled at them. To her Gar Quot was as bad as the rest, and she refused to fetch him beer. When he rose from a chair, Berthe would apply the fly spray implying that the area needed disinfecting. On the other hand she loved the Nuer children and tried to help with the morning sick parades, but the men would not be touched by her and even the women now preferred Rial Nyang!

Kor Jum also paid a visit to our camp, arriving early in the morning with his brother. They waited outside while I washed and shaved at leisure unaware that they were there. The prophet was not at all put out by this cavalier treatment, for he realized that our Amhara did not recognize his importance. Doereding had taken the day, or rather the night, off to stay with 'an aunt'. (His aunt turned out to be about 15 years old and very attractive, when I caught sight of her later in the day). Kor Jum and his brother came into the tent bearing a small bowl of butter. As Doereding was absent and there was no one else to interpret, I failed to understand what he wanted. My shirt was removed and delicately he rubbed the butter on my chest, behind my ears, and under my arms. Still seeming somewhat dissatisfied with the result, he took me by the hand and we set out on foot towards the village of Wiu. Thomas and Berthe wanted to come along too but Kor Jum waved his spear aggressively at them, indicating that they had better remain where they were.

Wiu was just the same; friendly voices shouted out a welcome to us. I was led straight to the hut containing the sacred spear and all three of us entered. There I was given a full blessing, which was later explained to me by Doereding. The prophet wanted me to marry, to be happy and to have many children. He also wanted me always to be a 'man of peace' and he hoped that, should anything happen to him, I would keep peace in the area. "In Lare, where the Nuer move during the rainy season, the people will build you a house. You will have land, cattle and wives. You can always live with us, Rial Nyang." When I came out of that house there was not a part of my anatomy that had not been buttered!

Doereding was waiting, having been sent for by the prophet to explain the message to me. I replied that I must return to England, to my real home. Kor Jum nodded understandingly, but insisted that someday I should come back again to the Nuer. "We will be waiting for you Rial Nyang. Do not forget us. For our people are being persecuted and we need your help." The prophet of Deng arrived and joining Kor Jum asked me to remain. I promised that I would come back someday; meanwhile that I should try to tell the world about the Nuer refugees and the war the Anya-Nya were fighting against the Arabs of North Sudan. Kor Jum wanted me to write a letter, saying that I had found him a good man and a man of peace. The prophet was only too aware that eager missionaries, angry police or envious governments might try to lock up the only real leader of these people. Without a leader the Nuer might more easily succumb to the advances of civilization or be robbed of their land and cattle. I wrote that letter of testimony in English and French, whilst Doereding translated it into Nuer and Amharic. All the documents were then solemnly placed together in a leather pouch and taken into the temple of Wiu, where I believe they remain today, together with a Wilkinson Sword Jungle Knife which I gave the prophet. Insofar as possible, they are my own blessing on the Nuer and my own prayer for their survival.

On the way back to camp, accompanied by Doereding, we stopped in a village where a row had just started. A good-looking and slightly frail youth about 10 years old, fully garred and therefore a man, was trying to stop an 18-year-old bully from taking away a fish which he had caught in the river. The other had no right to it, but by sheer strength had removed it and was now making off with the prize. The younger child was near to tears, but as the other galloped away, he made a grave mistake—he cursed him in the name of Wiu. "May Wiu take you", he shouted. This was serious, for it meant they must fight it out. What was equally serious was that the boys came from different villages, and a battle between them ending in the possible death of one or other could spark off nothing less than a village war.

I could not believe that these youngsters really meant to fight over such a trivial matter until I saw them running together towards the river. First they had a wrestling match where the elder roughed up the younger terribly. There was blood pouring from the child's nose and scratches and cuts on his body as they rolled naked on the earth, twisting, punching and biting. But despite the thumping he was getting, the young boy refused to give in. I wanted to intervene but was told by Doereding to stay out, since it had 'not yet become serious'. After a while, the combatants ceased, and exhausted went to wash in the river. I was about to go, thinking it was all over, when I saw the boys moving off with their spears. They were going to fight until one killed the other; yet, no one seemed prepared to stop them. Obviously, they did not wish to be watched by me.

Doereding and I gave chase, catching up with them just as the fighting began. "Quick," said Doerding, "you must stop them Rial Nyang in the name of Kor Jum and Wiu, for the prophet has given you the power of peace." I have done many weird things in my life but the next move I made was the strangest of all. Without hesitation, I rushed between the two boys. Both their spears remained pointed at me. They froze to the spot with astonishment at the intervention of a white man. Then very gently I disarmed first one then the other. I asked Doereding to tell both to sit on the ground side by side—and I laid a hand on each. "May your God or mine keep you two in peace," I muttered. A crowd had gathered by now, and I handed the spears to relatives of the boys who had at last turned up. As I walked away, Doereding clasped my hand with emotion. "You have done a wonderful thing," he said, "the people are praising you and saying you are a true son of Kor Jum. One thing is now certain—those boys will never fight each other again, for I told them that Rial Nyang had forbidden it." The power of peace had worked or else my presence as a white man had had the same effect. I had 'walked between spears' just as the prophet had done so many times, with no one harming him.

On the second day of the Baro river camp, we went for a crocodile shoot. Whatever Thomas' other failings, he is a great white hunter. It was mainly due to him that the very rare Nile Lechwe were found in Ethiopia. Elephant, pig, buffalo, gazelle, water buck and every other species of game available could and would be traced by this ingenious Yugoslav. Above all, he was

Two men enjoy seeds cooked in hot ashes

(*left*) House building.
(*below*) Rope making

known in the area as the crocodile man. At one time, he had held the crocodile licence on the Ghilo river and was reputed to have shot, speared or otherwise killed one thousand a month—an almost incredible number, considering he had to work with untrained teams of Anuak. He had also wrestled with crocodile in the water, clinging to their underbellies or riding on their backs. No doubt these stories were somewhat exaggerated by the natives, but then they must have had some elements of truth.

We picked a nice-looking reptile dozing on a bank and I shot it clear above the eyes into the brain—a rear shot made possible by a slight elevation of the head. The Anuak rushed forward and were skinning the crocodile while it was still twitching in after-death muscular reaction. It was a splendid specimen measuring just over 15 feet, so we saved most of it—in other words the soft skin of the under-belly, the head, the feet (they can be made into ashtrays) and even the back. The stomach was cut open and in it were found Anuak and Nuer beads, the only remains of previous victims. I felt no sorrow at killing these man-eating beasts.

It was time to break camp. Rial Nyang was now scrubbed, shaved, dressed and rapidly becoming a typical hunter on safari—another tourist. One or two objects of little value were found missing for the first time. Nothing of mine had ever been touched in Gwal Diok, but here a different code of conduct prevailed, and it was too easy for a thief to steal from Europeans. After all, Nuer village law would not apply. There would be no retribution, and anyway, the foreigners were rich. Berthe was all the more convinced that the Nuer were thieves and cut-throats. Whilst camp was being packed up and the tents and equipment loaded onto the vehicles, she armed herself with a stick hitting out at any tribesmen who got too near. Why on earth they took it I shall never know. I tried to restrain her, only to be told that if I had my way the Nuer would be able to steal everything and then murder us. Perhaps this Amharic female really was afraid, for I have seen Ethiopian police behave in a similar manner when hopelessly outnumbered by potential enemies.

All of this was destroying my relationship with the people, almost as fast as it had been created. I could not watch such treatment of those I genuinely admired for their qualities of courage, cheerfulness and, yes, honesty—amongst themselves. So I walked to Wiu and saw Kor Jum for the last time. Kiir turned up unexpectedly and after a while we wandered back to the scene of turmoil together, hand in hand, according to the African habit of friendship. The scene at the camp site was complete chaos and getting worse. Doereding had gone off on another romantic expedition so I could not rely on his help. By now over one hundred Nuer were enjoying the game of jeering at Berthe as she charged about with her stick, working herself into a frenzy. The children would chase her, shrieking; even some of the men rushed forward, grabbed an article before retreating—often only to throw the captured item back into the circle again. It was all a game, although undoubtedly some of Thomas' equipment was being lost in the process.

The time had come to act. I told Thomas to hurry up his crew and be ready to leave. I put Berthe out of harm's way in one of the trucks. Finally, taking a Nuer spear in my hand, I let it be known we were leaving. I still commanded just enough respect for this to work. Doereding arrived at the last minute and leapt into the truck as we drove off.

In this rather sad way, we left the Nuer; Kiir standing amongst the crowd, clutching a pair of my shorts and a shirt that he had always admired. Gar Quot had inherited my torch and Thiwat my underpants. The return journey seemed endless. Bumping along dirt tracks beside the river we made our way back towards Gambela. The rains had made the route treacherous. Once we had to go back to winch the second vehicle out of a ditch. Sometimes we stopped for coffee provided by Berthe, now as happy as a sandboy at the prospect of returning to Addis. At Pokwo we stopped at the mission station, but word travels fast in Africa, and the story of my pagan sacrifices had already reached them. If the missionaries were critical of me, I was equally appalled to find them charging the Anuak fees for medicine and treatment. It seemed better to disagree and go one's own way—for I have great respect for the civilizing work done by these 'men of God'—its just that it is not my way or my mission.

The rains came down in torrents and we could hardly see the route. The trucks churned through the mud, often getting stuck but eventually being dug out. In a day or two, this route would be impassable again until the dry season in September or October. When the convoy reached Gambela, it was two o'clock in the morning. It was still raining and the town was asleep. To save erecting tents in the rain and the dark, we slept in Thomas' shed, where he kept numerous skins of slaughtered buffalo. The smell was overpowering and the arrival of dawn was welcomed by the mixed company in the shed—half a dozen wet, muddy and sweaty Africans, two white men and Berthe. Dawn also brought other surprises—even before breakfast. Two armed Ethiopian policemen appeared at the door and hauled Thomas off to the police station. He tried to delay and was furious at being taken away like this in front of a client. It was, he said, bad for his image! Nevertheless the police had their orders. I next saw my white hunter for fifteen minutes which he took off from his court case—some local argument about rent—still accompanied by two policemen. Thomas had insisted on saying goodbye to me, his client, in proper fashion and had arrived to take me to the airport. The fact that he had left in the middle of his case with the court still in session awaiting his return, did not seem unusual. Nor was he unduly perturbed by the presence of the law at his side.

Addis Ababa was unchanged. The girls in the 'Queen of Sheba' still glistened as they twisted to Western pop, subdued lights shone on the monkey skins on the walls, and the same faces surrounded the bar. It was a time for swapping tales with John Blower and one of his game wardens, for drinking whisky and absorbing the atmosphere, smoky though it was. I was due to leave for London on Sunday morning, but first I had a note to send to the British Embassy and a courtesy call to make on HIH the Crown Prince, who had been kind to me on a previous visit. There was just time to attend Mass, for I managed to catch a service *en route* for the airport. The priest was mumbling away; there had been incense in the Church; the congregation was a mixture of races, but mostly Amhara or American. My hands tingled as the feeling of power began to depart—the power to impart health and peace. Rial Nyang was being cut down to size. The words of the Mass became reality—"*Dominus Vobiscum—Et Cum spirito tuo*"—"*Ite Missa est.*" So, with the last blessing over, I was returning to the destructive civilized world we all struggle so hard to create.

The War of Survival

APPENDIX I

In the text only brief references have been made to the battles of the Nuer and their political persecution. These people, now totalling some 400,000, are nomadic pastoralists, who, according to the season, follow the grazing of their cattle; boundaries have little or no meaning. Many Nuer are both Ethiopian and Sudanese, living part of the year in each country. This applies particularly to the eastern clans who inhabit the lands around the Ghilo and Baro rivers in Ethiopia, stretching to Nasir and Jokau in the Sudan. It is possible to talk of the troubles in the Sudan with Anya-Nya representatives who freely wander amongst the refugees in Ethiopia and Uganda. Yet these same men who have dedicated themselves to a war of independence may be back across the border and in the thick of the battle a few hours later, proving that borders only exist in the minds of police, army and politicians.

Let us go back in history to the days of British administration prior to Independence. The present Arab government in Khartoum would have us believe that foreign missionary activity was a mask assumed to conceal political and imperialistic objectives. Successive Arab governments have claimed that the British encouraged the south to develop along separate lines to the north in order to create divisions which had not previously existed. This is untrue. Long before the foreigners came, the native inhabitants, being mainly Nilotic negroes in the South, differed in religion, character, occupation and colour from the Moslem Arabs of the north. The British administration, far from being a divisive force, brought a certain amount of law and order to the south, making it possible for the missions to fulfill their functions as educators.

In retrospect one could claim that not enough was done, but when you consider the difficult conditions under which these good people worked, it is truly amazing what they accomplished. Even if Christianity was not always acceptable, education and medicine were welcomed. Thus prior to the independence of the Sudan much had already been accomplished in the south. Always remember that these primitive and pagan peoples had their own traditions, customs and trading systems, although in a less advanced form than the Arabs in the north. Five million people inhabited this area of the Nile basin containing the vast swamp of the 'Sud' but also other and more fertile land. Compared with this, 7 million inhabited the more sandy desert areas of the North. (A recent report by the minority Rights Group entitled "The Southern Sudan and Eritrea" estimates the population of the Sudan as 16 million, with only 4 million left in the south.)

To some the independence of the Sudan was to be the great experiment; the conclusive proof that Arab and negroid peoples could live together in harmony in a single state. The British administrators were not so starry-eyed (see Appendix 2). Many of those who strongly objected to the eventual handover of the Sudan could ill afford to forfeit the pensions which would in future be paid, not by the British but the Khartoum government. Neighbouring African states are still today reluctant to admit that the Sudan has failed, for they fear the implications of Afro-Arab conflict. It is important for the continent of Africa that this should be avoided but it is equally important that the leaders in Africa today should realize that suppression of minorities is no solution. The OAU may close its eyes and claim the right of non-intervention in the internal affairs of the African nations, but surely the United Nations has a duty to perform.

Self-rule was granted to the Sudan in 1954, and Mr E. Azhari became the first Prime Minister. The south was represented by twenty-two members of parliament who found themselves powerless to secure the promotion of southerners to posts in the army, as district commissioners or government officials. In July 1955 twenty demonstrators at Yambio were shot. This was followed by further incidents, and in August 1955 the revolutionary force was founded. The south was still hoping for some kind of federal solution when the British Governor General departed from office. The Sudan became independent in the eyes of the world on 1st January 1956, but southerners still ignore this date as meaningless; for them one master had merely been substituted for another. Even before this the army in the south was in revolt and many of the soldiers had fled into the bush. A state of emergency existed.

It is puzzling how in this atmosphere Britain granted Independence to the Sudan with so few safeguards to protect the southerner on whom they had previously lavished so much care and attention. Britain, I believe, still has a moral responsibility to the south. Had not the Suez crisis loomed so large on the international scene, perhaps the attitude of Her Majesty's Government might have been less propitiatory towards the aspirations of Khartoum. However, the real change in British Policy dates from 1947 when, at the conference held at Juba, it was decided to try to lay the basis of 'one nation' in the Sudan. It was already too late to change the course of history. By 1957 Abdalla Khalil was in power and demands from the south for federal status became overwhelming—so much so, that by November 1958 the Prime Minister had handed over the government to the army. From 1958–1964 a military regime was in power. Southerners were sentenced to death if found to be involved in politics. Villages were burned whilst politicians, students and soldiers alike took to the bush. General Abboud's government became increasingly unpopular as unemployment rose and the vast sums needed for crushing the rebellion became less readily available. Meanwhile, in the forests of the south, the early Anya-Nya was growing in strength—especially when this revolutionary army was able to acquire a large quantity of arms, both captured by them and sold to them at the time of the collapse of Simba's and the Congo Mercenaries. In 1964 the Abboud government was overthrown and Sir El Khatim became Prime Minister of the caretaker government but not before the last of the missionaries had been expelled.

As first the missionaries had kept the outside world in touch with what was happening, but then they discovered that their movements were being curtailed and so long as they remained in the South Sudan they were confined to their mission stations. One report from Khartoum stated categorically that the missionaries were standing between the Southern tribes people and the Southern Arabs, who are in fact the government. The army had taken over in November 1958 but the real pressure on the missionaries only came several years later with the nationalization of the mission schools and the change of the day of rest from Sunday to Friday. This was later reversed owing to the intense opposition in the South to Moslem laws, but resentment remained. Small government clinics were built in villages where the missions had medical work and when these buildings were completed the missions were ordered to close down. It therefore became increasingly impossible to carry on and by the early 1960s approximately 50 per cent of the Protestant missionary force in the Sudan had been expelled. The same was true of the Roman Catholics. By 1962 expulsions had gained momentum and over 65 per cent had been expelled whilst no replacements were allowed in. The curtain finally fell on the missions in 1964, when a government proclamation was first heard by some of them on the wireless: "Three hundred foreign missionaries from the Southern Sudan have been asked to leave the country." This was the news bulletin from the BBC; those on the spot had not yet received the expulsion order.

Missionary work was now considered a legacy of colonialism and police were despatched to all the mission stations to assist in the expulsion. Most of the missionaries who had spent a lifetime in the southern Sudan were given only a few hours to make their preparations to leave. However, after the missionaries had gone and the hospitals were closed, there were no European witnesses left. The few Greek and Syrians in the south were expelled at the same time. Students from the south were taken to colleges which had been transferred to the north and given an Arab education including instruction in the Koran and sometimes even circumcision—a disgrace amongst some Nilotic tribesmen. The idea was that these boys should then return to the south and attempt to convert others to Arab ways.

Resistance in the south meanwhile continued at an accelerated pace. The more pressure placed on the Southern tribesmen, the more they fought for their own survival. Tribes which for years had been traditional enemies came together and formed a provisional government which later sent an appeal for help to the United Nations. This government had representatives of the Nuer, Dinka, Bari, Anuak and many other tribes. It contained a number of graduates of the missionary schools who listed their religion after their names. At one time there was an almost equal balance in the provisional government between those trained by the Catholic missionaries and those by the Protestants. Later there were splits between the different groups. These divisions nearly caused the southern movement to degenerate into tribal rivalry.

Bands of rebels began to receive occasional supplies of arms and ammunition from outside although outside aid has been greatly exaggerated. As funds were short, the army was often expected to live off the land. Sometimes the rebels earned a bad name by plundering their own villages. Otherwise they chose as their targets for attack, police posts, army barracks and supply lines in the south, occasionally achieving remarkable success but at other times meeting with failure. The rebel leaders seldom united continued to wander, not only across the Southern Sudan, but also amongst the refugees now clustered across the borders of Congo, Chad, Kenya, Ethiopia, Uganda and the Central Africa Republic. Already these refugees numbered over 100,000. Soon the number was to increase to half a million.

Meanwhile, not all southerners had taken to the bush. Political movements continued to try to operate in Khartoum on behalf of their comrades, hoping that by political pressure they might achieve their ends. Both SANU and the Southern Front were political parties which kept apart from the Anya-Nya yet expressed a body of Southern opinion which believed that co-operation with Khartoum was possible. A few southerners became ministers in the Khartoum government, believing that by so doing they could help their people. One southerner in particular, William Deng, stood out as a leader and tried to negotiate peace, only to die mysteriously at the hands of the Northern army.

A serious attempt was made to find a solution in March 1965 under the premiership of Sir El Khatim at the round-table conference in Khartoum. This was suggested by the southern leaders who wanted to reach a workable programme of federation. Observers came from other African States and there was a tentative offer of some form of 'local autonomy' to the south. Even so the army in the south was strengthened, whilst mass killings at Warajok, Tonji and Gogrial took place. In June 1965 Mohammed Mahgoub came to power and swiftly undid any of the good achieved by the round-table conference. As a hard-liner he advocated attacks on educated southerners and often their imprisonment. In July 1965 hideous massacres at Juba and Wau took place. October 1966 brought Saddick el Mahdi to power, a young man who has often been described as a skilful politician. A descendant of the famous Mahdi who opposed General Gordon, he was certainly in a position to bring about a solution—but he failed to do so. Perhaps his powerful relatives and the Umma party dissuaded him. Indeed, somewhat surprisingly he maintained there no longer was a problem in the south. Mahgoub returned to power again in April 1967 and true to form continued a policy which to the eyes of many Southerners virtually amounted to genocide and Arab colonization.

The May 1969 revolution, it was hoped, would change everything. The revolutionary government offered 'autonomy'; but the exact implication is still unknown, and there is no evidence of any concrete achievements. Nor is it likely that missionaries will be back in force, or that vast sums (which are not available) will be spent on the education of the south. Southern politicians such as Joseph Garang, the late minister of southern affairs, had been working with Khartoum and had toured the refugee camps, trying to persuade the inmates to return. But these refugees had lived through too much persecution to trust others with their fate, especially previous members of the Communist Party! They had seen the Sudanese army set up machine guns in their villages to kill women and children indiscriminately. They had watched their homes being burned and their cattle stolen. Many of the educated southerners had at one time or another been under arrest.

Nasser's men vied with communist countries to influence Khartoum. Government in the Sudan prior to the 1969 coup reached rock bottom, for even the lives of Government ministers were in danger. Little could be done, therefore, to protect the tribesmen from the Sudanese army stationed there ostensibly to maintain law and order. As one authorative source in Khartoum said to me, "Life in a Southern village depends on the whims of the local military commander." The flood of refugees and their gruesome accounts of what was happening provided the only evidence to the outside world that all was not well, although the Khartoum government at first denied the existence of any trouble, let alone a full-scale war. The southern peoples, they said, were nomadic warriors, who had, in all probability, simply been fighting amongst themselves. The presence of refugees was, until recently, explained away as representing normal pastoral migrations. There was some truth in these allegations—just enough to ensure that the situation did not become an embarrassment to the neighbouring governments of the Congo, Uganda and Ethiopia—none of whom relished a total diplomatic break with Khartoum.

After January 1970 the situation became more serious. Far from offering 'autonomy' the Nimeiry government increased pressure on the south. There was evidence of the importation of Egyptian and Russian advisors, the bombing of southern villages by Egyptian piloted MIGs and the supply of funds from East Germany to Khartoum. The African states surrounding the Sudan became alarmed by the ever increasing flow of refugees arriving in their lands. Besides the Nile Provisional Government several other groups in the south had been established. Increasing evidence came to hand that foreign powers were becoming involved in supporting the rebels, who had abandoned any hope of reconciliation with Khartoum. In

July 1970 the Nile Provisional Government fell, as had the Anyidi some months before. The whole of the Southern Sudanese Resistance Movement then came under Colonel Joseph Lagu.

Numerous charitable concerns had begun to turn their attention towards helping the south Sudanese. In London an organization called the Southern Sudan Association was formed to publicise the southern viewpoint in a journal called *Grass Curtain*. This association attempted to link up with other groups which had arisen all over the world in Norway, Denmark, Switzerland, Canada, Sweden, Germany, Italy, France, Belgium and the USA. At last the unknown war in the south began to receive some publicity. The situation may yet escalate in an international sense only to bring increased hardship and retribution on innocent southerners. A solution to the southern problem is all the more important now that the Sudan's internal war has taken on, in miniature, the image of the Middle East conflict. After the attempted coup d'etat in the summer of 1971 Nimeiry's regime at first appeared to become dependent on aid from Egypt and Syria, thus moving further towards the Arab powers and away from Ethiopia, East Africa and the Congo. Was this an optical illusion?

Background to the Southern Sudan

APPENDIX 2

by Richard Owen
(formerly Governor of Bahr el Ghazal)
Reprinted from the *Grass Curtain*, August 1970

In 1953, shortly before leaving the Sudan, I was up in Khartoum, from Wau, the capital of Bahr el Ghazal Province, and met an Arab sheikh, an old friend. We greeted each other warmly and fell to it, having a grand chin-wag over old times. After half an hour he suddenly changed the subject, saying—"And what about the people down at Wau? They are all slaves, are they?"

In those few naive words lie a thousand years of history, and, whatever the frills and the varying degrees of responsibility, that sentence gave the fundamental cause of today's agony.

BRITAIN ESTABLISHES ORDER IN SOUTH SUDAN (1900–1955)

On pre-1900 history I will not touch, for I take it to be known. When Britain took responsibility for the Sudan in 1898, the Southern Provinces (Upper Nile, Bahr el Ghazal and Equatoria—then Mongalla) contained scores and scores of tribes, languages and customs; Bantu and Nilotic, ruined and reduced by slave-raiding, with no economy, no communications, no education and very little that one could call civilization. The first quarter of a century therefore went not in political advance but in establishing order out of chaos, confidence out of fear. The last patrol (against recalcitrant Nilotic Nuer) was in the late twenties, and thereafter the South was pacific; settled and directly administered by British, simple in texture, well content and quite uneconomic, financed from the more progressive North.

As a 'new boy' in 1926 I spent a year in Bahr el Ghazal. From 1936 to 1939, in the Civil Secretary's office, I saw Southern affairs 'from within'. In 1945 I went back as Deputy Governor to Bahr el Ghazal, which had been unwisely washed out as a province and left to rot. In 1948 I became Governor of the resuscitated Province.

On pre-war policy I speak with reserve. No Civil Secretary of the Sudan ever (I think) served in the South or ever at first hand understood its problems.

The Sudan was financially dependent on the British Treasury until 1923. It had to be made economic. The policy, pre-1939, always appeared to me to be (1) to concentrate effort and funds on the productive North, and in the South to mark time; (2) to remember that the South was African, not Arab, and, while not aiming at separation (since the South was in any case held to be an unviable entity), yet not to encourage contacts with the North, to encourage English as the language of the future, and to permit or even further controlled missionary work, as a civilizing and educative agency, so that the South might one day develop its own way. This policy has been abused and misrepresented, and may be open to criticism, but under the circumstances it was logical.

During the war it became apparent that Independence was much nearer than most of us ever guessed. The South had to be prepared for this. The result was a programme, almost a crash programme, of expenditure on education and on development (Dinka cattle trade, Zande Scheme for cotton and coffee, rice at Aweil, etc). Northern officials a-many were posted to help with this (and with a few exceptions regarded the South as exile). The Southern official was kept on less well-paid terms than the Northerners. This caused natural resentment, but in my experience was not wholly unjust, since the Southerner was for the most part less well educated, less sober and less reliable and therefore of inferior calibre. Some approach to parity was achieved in my time.

Anyway, the work went forward and great strides were made; and had independence come in 1965 instead of 1955, all might have been well. It is one of the 'mights' of history.

THE JUBA CONFERENCE

Meanwhile what of the political future? The South sensed that Independence was coming. Our memories are short; African ones are long; any middle-aged man could remember the slave-raiding days. Were they to be handed back, in the holy name of democracy, to their masters? There was nervousness and questioning. A number of us therefore asked the Central Government in 1946 for a conference, to allow Southern views to be put forward. This became known as "The Juba Conference". The Civil Secretary (Sir James Robertson) attended, the Governors and Deputy Governors of the three provinces, several influential Northern officials, and as representative an assortment (real democratic elected representation was impossible) of Southern chiefs, educated officials, etc, as could be mustered.

The first day the Southern view was stubborn and they would have no truck with the North nor any talk of final amalgamation. I could see the Civil Secretary was worried and rather desperate. There then occurred one of the most remarkable of volte-faces. Overnight, one of the Northern officials got hold of the educated Southern elements (omitting the chiefs) and by sheer genius of blarney talked them round, making promises, and pointing out that their only hope of parity and good jobs and a 'future' was to come in with the North.

Next day this educated element made it clear that they had changed their minds; and, despite the misgivings and mutterings of certain chiefs and others, it was agreed that the future of the South lay in unity with the North, granted a few safeguards and assurances of representation. I could see the immense relief of the Civil Secretary, and was left with the strongest impression that he had really come less to consult than to enforce a policy already decided by the Central Government.

Looking back, one can see that from that day the fate of the South was sealed. As Independence approached and forebodings in the South grew, so our warnings and protests to the Central Government increased. They were met with reassurances and with promises of 'safeguards' in the form of so many Southern seats in Parliament, so many ministries, and the power of appeal to the Governor General for his veto as long as a Governor General remained. . . . We felt then, and know now, that any such assurances were naive, since once British power was removed history and human nature would override all paper assurances.

In 1952 the three Southern Governors met and put up to the Central Government an outline scheme for Federation, leaving the South with a large measure of self-determination and a subordinate 'parliament' at Juba, while not splitting the country. We were politely thanked and no more was heard of it.

INDEPENDENCE APPROACHES

Finally, we were summoned to a meeting with Mr Selwyn Lloyd in Khartoum. He pointed out British policy; that any hint of separation (or of temporarily retaining British administration in the South) would be intensely resented by the North, would throw the North into the arms of Egypt, and thereby queer the pitch for the deal over Suez which Great Gritain hoped to make. The Southern Governors did their best to press the fears and forebodings of the South, the disastrous results locally of the proposed policy, and the absolute need for something more than paper safeguards which would be ineffective. No impression was made. Once only I saw Selwyn Lloyd really rattled, when I quoted an Embassy document which (indiscreetly shown to us no doubt) said that "we must, of course, ensure that the interests of the Southerners do not suffer by the proposed policy", a statement which, literally interpreted, would have meant sending British troops to aid the South even during the first mutiny of 1956–1957. The rest is history.

IN RETROSPECT—A TRAGEDY

Unless you are morbid, there is no joy in being a Cassandra. All that we had predicted came to pass, and much more. The British idea of unifying a country is to leave minorities plenty of rein and as much self-determination as possible, and to let the parts grow together. The Arab idea is diametrically the opposite, and based on the motto "Cujus Regio, Ejus Religio"—a unity coerced by one language, one civilization, one religion.

Against this the Africans, shackled by division of tribe and language, by distance and by lack of educated leaders, had no defence save intense resentment and a determination to be African, not Arab (and in many cases Christian, not Muslim). The strife, the horror, the bloodshed, the racial hatred that has existed since then, I naturally know at second hand, not first hand, and therefore will not enter upon. The charge against the North of 'genocide' (an abused and exaggerated word) is true in so far as Khartoum governments, or the Northern soldiers with their connivance, did make a bid to liquidate educated elements and potential leaders as a matter of policy.

Factual stories of the ghastly details I will leave to others. But the above shows the political background to what has become one of the tragedies of the modern world.

Policy Statement on the Southern Question

APPENDIX 3

(A poster nailed to trees in the south for the people to read)
(Issued by the Nimeiry Government in Khartoum)
August 1969

Dear Countrymen,

Warm congratulations and greetings to you on this historic occasion of your Revolution.

No doubt you have heard of the broad aims of the Revolution outlined in my speech and in that of the Prime Minister which was broadcast on the 25th of May. Our Revolution is the continuation of the October 21 Popular Revolution. It works for the regeneration of life in our country, for social progress and the raising of the standard of living of the masses of our people throughout the country. It stands against imperialism, colonialism and whole-heartedly supports the liberation movements of the African and Arab peoples as well as other peoples throughout the world.

A HISTORICAL BACKGROUND

Dear Countrymen,

The revolutionary Government is fully aware of the magnitude of the Southern problem and is determined to arrive at a lasting solution.

This problem has deep-going historical roots dating back to the last century. It is the result of the policies of British colonialism which left the legacy of uneven development between the Northern and Southern parts of the country, with the result that on the advent of Independence Southerners found themselves in an unequal position with their Northern brethren in every field.

The traditional circles and parties that held the reins of power in our country since Independence have utterly failed to solve the

Southern question. They have exploited state power for self-enrichment and for serving narrow partisan interests without caring about the interests of the masses of our people whether in the North or in the South.

It is important to realize also that most of the Southern leaders contributed a great deal to the present deterioration of the state of affairs in that part of our beloved country. Over the years, since 1950 to the present day they have sought alliances with the Northern reactionary circles and with imperialism, whether from inside or outside the borders. Personal gain was the mainspring of their actions.

Dear Countrymen,

The enemies of the North are also the enemies of the South. The common enemy is imperialism and neo-colonialism which is oppressing and exploiting the African and Arab peoples, and standing in the way of their advance. Internally, our common enemies are the reactionary forces of counter-revolution. The 25 May Revolution is not the same as the coup d'etat of November 1958. That was a reactionary move staged by the imperialists in alliance with local reaction in and outside the army. It was made to silence the demands of the masses of our people in both the North and the South for social change and genuine democracy.

The Revolution of May 25th is the very opposite of the coup d'etat of 1958. Our Revolution is, we repeat, directed against imperialism, the reactionary circles and corrupt parties that destroyed the October Revolution and were aiming at finally liquidating any progressive movement and installing a reactionary dictatorship.

Dear Countrymen,

The Revolutionary Government is confident and competent enough to face existing realities. It recognizes the historical and cultural differences between the North and South and firmly believes that the unity of our country must be built upon these objective realities. The Southern people have the right to develop their respective cultures and traditions within a united socialist Sudan.

In furtherance of these objectives the Revolutionary Council and the Council of Ministers held joint meetings and after a full discussion of the matter resolved to recognize the right of the Southern people to regional autonomy within a United Sudan.

REGIONAL AUTONOMY PROGRAMME

Dear Countrymen,

You will realize that the building of a broad socialist oriented democratic movement in the South, forming part of the revolutionary structure in the North and capable of assuming the reins of power in that region and rebuffing imperialist penetration and infiltration from the rear is an essential pre-requisite for the practical and healthy application of regional autonomy.

Within this framework and in order to prepare for that day when this right can be exercised the revolutionary Government is drawing up the following programme:

(1) The continuation and further extension of the Amnesty Law.
(2) Economic, social and cultural development of the South.
(3) The appointment of a Minister for Southern affairs and,
(4) The training of personnel.

The Government will create a special economic planning board for the South and will prepare a special budget for the South, which aims at the development of the Southern Provinces in the shortest possible time.

Dear Southern Countrymen,

In order that we may be able to carry out this programme it is of the utmost importance that peace and security should prevail in the South and that life return to normal. It is primarily the responsibility of you all whether you be in the bush or at home to maintain peace and stability. The way is open for those abroad to return home and co-operate with us in building a prosperous Sudan, united and democratic.

August 1969
Printed by Government Printing Press.

(Comment by the author:

After this declaration was issued and pinned to trees in the south for the population to read, the situation in southern Sudan deteriorated. Refugees flooded across the borders with tales of persecution, bombing of villages, torture of prisoners, burning of churches. If imperialism was once the common enemy, then the arrival of the Russians on the scene with MIG 17s, helicopters and advisers to assist Khartoum—can have done little to help. A full-scale guerilla war took place. Autonomy for the south appeared to have been but a dream!)

Autonomy for the South?

APPENDIX 4

WHAT HAS THE GOVERNMENT DONE SINCE MAY 1969?

EXTRACTS FROM A PRESS CONFERENCE: held on Monday, 20th April 1970, in Khartoum, by Joseph Garang, Minister for Southern Affairs, Khartoum Government.

"ACTION NOT WORDS"

"It is true that we declared a sound policy for the South. But what matters is the implementation of that Policy. What is important is what every Minister did to execute its part of the plans and projects. Action is not going on with the required speed. Implementation of this fiscal year's programmes including rice, coffee, etc is not going on with the required speed. All of us inside and outside must do so.

"Only with achievements which the ordinary Dinka and Nuer sees before his eyes can we rebut imperialist propaganda. I, therefore, suggest that my Minister colleagues, who have not seen the South, should go there to see if the work is going on satisfactorily or not."

Question by one journalist: "What has happened to implement regional autonomy?"

Answer: "The implementation is subject to certain prerequisites contained in 9th June Declaration. These include economic development, a competent cadre and the building of a democratic movement. This is what we are trying to do and hope to finish quickly."

Extract from the *Sudan News*,
Khartoum, April 1970.

(Comment by the author)

GENERAL POINTS

1 The south has been promised autonomy on many occasions: it has never been implemented.

2 The situation under the present government until recently has actually been worse than it ever was before in the eyes of the southerners because:

a The Khartoum government has called for Egyptian troops to be trained in the Sudan. A Russian Ideological training school has also been established in Wad Seina.

b The intervention of foreign aircraft: for the first time Egyptian-manned Russian-built MIGs have bombed civilians in the South.

c With the unrest in the north, the massacre of the Mahdi and a number of his followers, it is inconceivable that the Khartoum government could risk recalling the army from the south—thus putting numerous soldiers out of a job. There is too much discontent and unemployment already to risk another military revolt.

d Many people in the south originally believed the government was sincere in its offer of autonomy, some refugees returned and others came out of the bush. The population near the towns grew, especially in the 'peace camps' where the residents can only enter and exit with passes, and hostages are frequently gathered together and shot as reprisals for Anya-Nya attacks. Soon those who returned were disillusioned.

e Since October 1969 the flood of refugees fleeing from the south has increased owing to deteriorating living conditions and persecution.

f The government has declared that Arabic will be taught in all schools—thus paying no attention to the preference of southerners who were previously taught in their local dialect or in English.

g Outside the main southern towns there is little medicine or education available for the local population. The tribesmen fear the sudden and often inexplicable attacks by the Arab soldiers. Khartoum has little control over the army.

h Those southerners assisting the Khartoum government are not men respected by their people. Joseph Garang, for instance, had little success in persuading the refugees in Uganda, the Congo, Ethiopia, the Central African Republic and Kenya to return. He was then shot by his colleagues. The United Nations refugee camps alone are populated by over 200,000 South Sudanese at this moment. Many more tribesmen have simply crossed the borders and settled in neighbouring lands alongside the local population—thus bringing our estimate of the number of refugees outside the Sudan up to 500,000. This takes no account of those people detained in the 'peace camps' inside or those taken to the north.

IS THERE A SOLUTION?

Short of a complete independence it is hard to see a solution. The divisions are caused by racial, religious and cultural differences between the Muslim, Arab northerners and the Pagan or Christian Negroid southerners.

However, perhaps by informing the general public of what is really happening in South Sudan today we can:

1 Shame the Khartoum regime into desisting from attempting genocide.
2 Force a recall of troops from the south.
3 Urge a meeting of southern leaders with the government to agree the terms of a real 'federal autonomy'—such a meeting to be held on neutral ground. (This has already been requested by the Anya-Nya leaders and is supported by the churches.)
4 Arrange for the repatriation of refugees.
5 Request permission for the return of the missionaries, expelled in 1964, with permission for them to re-open their hospitals. (The present government declared this intention, but so far there is little evidence of African missionaries being allowed any freedom. Most of those who went back have had to leave again.)
6 Request that aid be allowed to be distributed in the south by international organizations such as the Red Cross, Oxfam, United Nations etc, with local independent observers present. Above all such aid must reach the countryside and not remain in the towns only. Nor should it be used for political purposes or be looked upon as a gift from Khartoum.

Only by such swift action will it be possible to avoid the escalation of the southern Sudanese problem with foreign powers becoming involved. Further, it would be advisable in this context for the Khartoum government to dispense with the services of Russian, Egyptian and Libyan mercenaries.

Lastly should any solution be reached between north and south Sudan, let there be effective supervision by the United Nations, so that peace is assured and justice guaranteed.

Recent Events

APPENDIX 5

At the time of going to press developments are taking place which may lead to a solution by the granting of federal status to South Sudan.

The 1971 attempted coup d'etat doubtless startled the Nimeiry regime into eliminating communist influence. The Khartoum Government, after the attempted coup had failed, began strenuously to seek a Southern solution and, supported by international bodies as well as by representatives of the neighbouring countries, negotiations were commenced. It is still too early to predict whether a lasting solution can be reached but for the first time in over 15 years there is perhaps reason for cautious optimism.

As a result of the publicity which has recently been given to the war in the South by the world press and to the unification of the Southern Sudanese Liberation Movement under Joseph Lagu, it became possible for the Movement as a whole and for the Anya-Nya in particular, to appoint representatives who in the early months of 1972 met with the representatives of the Khartoum Government in order to seek a solution. This hopefully has been found.

Joseph Garang is dead but the present Vice-President and Minister for Southern Affairs, Mr Abel Alier, enjoys considerable Southern support and has been energetically pressing forward with schemes for the inclusion of Southerners in Government, diplomatic and civil posts and for increasing economic aid to the South. Perhaps history is in the making and common sense will overcome previous racial prejudice between Arab and African. Self-rule for South Sudan is no longer a dream; it could become reality.

Addis Ababa
February, 1972

Index

Index